the
Olive Harvest
Cookbook

the
Olive Harvest
Cookbook

Olive Oil Lore and Recipes from the McEvoy Ranch

GERALD GASS
with Jacqueline Mallorca

Foreword by
JOYCE GOLDSTEIN

Photographs by
MAREN CARUSO

Introduction by
NAN TUCKER McEVOY

CHRONICLE BOOKS
SAN FRANCISCO

Library of Congress Cataloging-in-Publication Data
available.

ISBN 0-8118-4162-6

Manufactured in Hong Kong.

DESIGNED BY BENJAMIN SHAYKIN
COMPOSITION BY KRISTEN WURZ
TYPESET IN HIGHTOWER, TRADE GOTHIC, AND SUTRO
PROP STYLING BY MAREN CARUSO, KIM KONECNY,
   AND ERIN QUON
FOOD STYLING BY KIM KONECNY AND ERIN QUON
PHOTO ASSISTANT: FAIZA ALI

Distributed in Canada by Raincoast Books
9050 Shaughnessy Street
Vancouver, British Columbia V6P 6E5

10 9 8 7 6 5 4 3 2 1

Chronicle Books LLC
85 Second Street
San Francisco, California 94105

www.chroniclebooks.com

Contents

Foreword

NAN MCEVOY IS ONE OF MY HEROINES. I ADMIRE her forthrightness, her sense of visual style, her taste in art and architecture, and her dedication to the environment. McEvoy Ranch is a stunning and dramatic place where all of these attributes come together. In her late seventies, an age when most people would be retired, retrenching and retreating from public life, she started a business and has not looked back.

When she bought the Petaluma property for her family, she learned that in order to make any major improvements the ranch had to be used for agricultural purposes. To comply, she could have bought a couple of horses and a goat and called it a day. But she had a vision. A vision of Tuscany superimposed on the rolling hills of Northern California. She planted 18,000 Italian olive trees with the goal of producing the finest possible organic olive oil using artisanal methods. And she has succeeded. The oil is superb and highly prized by chefs and dedicated home cooks.

I met Nan McEvoy and her family when I had my San Francisco restaurant, Square One. They were frequent diners and enjoyed our Mediterranean-inspired cuisine. Our paths are now intertwined in a wonderful confluence of events. Lucky for me, her son, Nion, became my publisher. The brilliant landscape designer who planned the ranch and the gardens is Patrick Brennan, one of our Square One waiters who took a leave of absence to travel and came back to a major career change and revealed an artist's soul. The chef at McEvoy Ranch is Gerald Gass. Gerald worked with me as a sous chef at Square One for five years. He loved cooking Mediterranean food. We tasted and talked about food all the time. We put up thousands of jars of preserves together. I was heartbroken when he gave notice, but he longed to move his young family to the country.

When Nan called and said she was looking for someone to cook at the ranch, I recommended Gerald. I knew that she and Gerald would hit it off. He is possessed of a quiet manner, a dry sense of humor, and a sense of loyalty. He is passionate about good ingredients, a diligent cook, and well-versed in olive oil–based Mediterranean food. The first time I visited, when Gerald was cooking lunch in that wonderful ranch kitchen, I knew that this was a perfect fit. His face, when he gave me a tour through the kitchen garden, told the story. He was in culinary heaven. The superb recipes in this book show the marriage of first-rate organic ingredients with a cook's refinement and skill. With his clear thinking, his sense of organization, and his discerning palate, he produces food with great taste and a simple but elegant style with nothing superfluous. Whenever I am homesick for Italy I just need to get in my car, visit McEvoy Ranch, and taste the food anointed with their fabulous olive oil. Nan's vision has been brought to fruition.

—*Joyce Goldstein*

Introduction

I DID NOT SET OUT TO BE AN OLIVE GROWER. What I originally wanted was a country retreat where I could spend more time with my son, Nion, and his three children. In short, I wanted a place where my grandchildren could run about just as I had done as a child on my family's ranch in Oregon.

In 1990, after a bit of a search, I acquired 550 acres in western Marin County, an easy drive across the Golden Gate Bridge from my home in San Francisco. The land was zoned strictly for agricultural use, so I had to come up with a bona fide agricultural purpose before I could make any improvements. Northern California was already heavily planted in wine grapes, and I knew nothing about making wine. But the grapevine's Mediterranean companion, the olive tree, was a definite possibility. I have always loved olive oil. Inspired by Maggie Blyth Klein's book *The Feast of the Olive*, I flew to Italy to meet one of her advisors, Dr. Maurizio Castelli . . . and came home with one thousand baby Tuscan olive trees.

Of course, it wasn't quite as simple as that. The decision to plant olives was made only after touring a number of olive groves in Italy and asking a lot of questions. I also had lengthy consultations with Dr. Castelli, an enologist who is also one of Italy's top olive oil production experts. And having made my decision, I had to transform a run-down dairy ranch into something else altogether.

The roof on the original 1880s farmhouse leaked like a sieve, with disastrous results. The farm buildings that were clustered in the center of the property had a common theme: they had either fallen down or threatened collapse. Sagging barbed-wire fences did little to prevent the incumbent cows from wandering off down the road.

In order to protect my young olive trees from deer, one of the first things I did was have the future orchards surrounded by an eight-foot-high deer fence. A navigable gravel road replaced rutted tracks, and Monterey cypresses and poplars were planted as windbreaks. The first hillside orchard was laid out, with irrigation installed for each olive tree, and tons of gypsum, lime, crushed oyster shell, and compost were added to improve the heavy clay soils.

At the same time, a building program was under way. Whenever possible, old barns were repaired and given a new lease on life, but in one case a derelict building was such a ruin that I called the local fire department and asked if the firemen would like to set it ablaze for a practice session. They responded with enthusiasm.

In addition, completely new structures were needed for living, for guests, for entertaining all my hoped-for olive oil buyers, and for the *frantoio*, or "olive mill," a building that would also house the ranch shop and business offices, a job that I turned over to interior designer Michael Booth and architect Marc Appleton. In addition, I commissioned landscape designer Patrick Brennan to come up with an overall plan. His vision has completely transformed the appearance of the ranch, and he continues to act as a consultant today. It was he who recommended reorienting my proposed house to face one of the five large ponds that are central to the farm's existence. (They catch winter runoff used for irrigation during the rest of the year.) In time, the view from the house, originally of sun-scorched hillsides, would also encompass row upon row of graceful olive trees, a sight that never fails to delight me. Patrick and stonemason George Gonzales together designed the low stone landscaping walls that accent the whole site. George builds them by hand, which is an art in itself.

I wanted to save the dilapidated Victorian farmhouse, but it was too far gone. Instead, an exact replica was constructed on a new site, minus all the additions that had been tacked on over the years, but using much of the original millwork. The current "Victorian," as I call it, is used for special events. It is one of a number of buildings scattered around a stone courtyard; others include a large meeting room with a big fireplace, a pavilion, and a children's center. The old dairy barn has become a greenhouse for olive seedlings. As the orchard grew, new plantings from cuttings of the original one thousand trees were made, and today there are some eighteen thousand trees in the ground. With the orchard capacity reached, the ranch now sells five thousand baby trees to the public each year, all of them propagated from the original "parent" trees, along with McEvoy Ranch's organic extra virgin olive oil, olive oil soap, and honey.

On the far side of the courtyard lies the big country kitchen, a welcoming space with profes-sional appliances along one wall separated from the long dining table by a thirteen-foot maple-topped island. One of the few non-native trees that was on the property when I bought it, an English walnut, shades the deck outside and provides a generous crop each year. I have lunch with ranch staff members here as often as I can; it's a nice way to conduct business meetings. A wood-burning bread oven stands outside, at the edge of the kitchen garden. Chefs Gerald Gass and Mark Rohrmeier make the most wonderful country loaves in it every day. What we eat for lunch is dictated by whatever is at its peak in the garden; we're strictly seasonal.

The first olive seedlings were planted in 1992; the mature date palms and ornamental palm trees that "anchor" the home site soon followed, and the kitchen garden was laid out. Today, a decade later, great cascades of flowering plants frame all the buildings and landscaping walls. As an afterthought, we put in ground-level lighting to illuminate the pathways—it was as black as pitch out there on a moonless night. The house is now surrounded by eighty acres of silvery-green olive trees that supply an ever-increasing harvest of organic extra virgin oil each year.

Last but not least, my grandchildren adore the ranch, as I had hoped they would. Becoming an olive grower turned out to be a sterling idea.

Nan Tucker McEvoy

Olive Growing in California

LOCATED IN THE ROLLING HILLS OF WESTERN Marin County, the McEvoy Ranch was once part of a Spanish land grant, a connection that is bound up in the history of California. Briefly put, back in the days when present-day California was part of Mexico and therefore under the Spanish crown, Spain wanted to protect her holdings there from other world powers by encouraging settlement of her own choosing. The Spanish then living in Mexico were reluctant to leave their secure lives, so as an inducement, the crown decreed that large tracts of land could be granted to veteran soldiers in the hopes that they would become ranchers.

These massive *ranchos* were deeded with nothing more than a signed order accompanied by a crudely drawn map. Boundaries were sketchy at best. Decades later, when California was ceded by an independent Mexico to the United States, legal ownership was hotly contested and many of the original grant lands passed into the hands of later settlers.

Spanish expeditions had begun filtering into California from Mexico in the late 1500s, but it was not until 1769 that a group of Franciscan monks led by Father Junípero Serra established their first mission in San Diego. By 1824, twenty-one missions punctuated the Camino Real—"King's Highway"— a route that stretched northward as far as San Francisco. The final mission to be built, which still stands in the town of Sonoma, lies less than twenty miles from McEvoy Ranch.

In addition to planting crops, olive groves, vineyards, and orchards, the Franciscans grazed large herds of cattle to support a burgeoning hide and tallow industry. With native people acting both as converts and laborers, the missions controlled huge areas, and they introduced irrigation into what is essentially a semiarid land.

The first California olive oil ran from a press at Mission San Diego de Alcalá in 1803, but history doesn't relate how it tasted. The press was still in existence over a century later—it is mentioned in George Wharton James's *The Old Franciscan Missions of California*, published in 1913—but has long since disappeared, as have many of the graceful old adobe mission buildings themselves.

In 1834, a little more than a decade after Mexico declared independence from Spain, the Mexican government "secularized" the Franciscan missions, taking the land away from the church and attaching it to the colony of California. Forced to abandon their huge farms, the Franciscans were permitted to keep only church buildings and a few acres here and there for building schools. Without their care, the mission olive groves, grapevines, fruit trees, and vegetable gardens languished and soon deteriorated.

The colony slept in the sun, but not for long. In 1848, following the Mexican-American War, huge areas that included present-day California were ceded to the United States. In that same year, gold was discovered at Sutter's Creek. By 1851, San Francisco—entry point for gold seekers from all over the world—had exploded from a population of about eight hundred to over twenty thousand. The influx included many Italians looking for a better life, among them some from Lucca, a region that has long been celebrated for its olive oil. Their gold lust exhausted, these Italians settled down as farmers, mainly in the inland valleys. Many of them introduced seeds and cuttings from their homeland. Along with other crops, they planted olive trees so that they could make olive oil for their own use and sell or barter any surplus.

By the 1870s, olive oil was being manufactured commercially by enterprising ranchers who had hit upon the idea of taking thousands of cuttings from hardy old Mission olive trees—trees that had survived unaided for decades. Olive oil made from the Mission olive was suddenly big business. Unfortunately, it had to compete with imported low-cost (and, it must be said, frequently rancid or adulterated) olive oil from various Mediterranean countries, where growers had also heard about California's growing market. Domestically produced cottonseed and other vegetable oils were responsible for even more competition. These cheap, bland cooking oils were marketed aggressively across the country, and American housewives who were not first-generation Mediterranean immigrants quickly became accustomed to them.

Swamped by cheaper European imports, supplies of California olive oil soon dwindled to a trickle, but table olives began to gain attention. Cured olives had always been part of the Spanish and Italian diet, but now, in the first decade of the twentieth century, new canning methods could be used to produce a mild-tasting, less "foreign" product that would appeal to a mass market. It did. The ubiquitous canned ripe black Mission olive was born, and still accounts for a lion's share of the California olive industry.

Happily, commercial olive oil production in California did not vanish altogether. In 1952, Ancel Keys, the father of modern nutrition, initiated his most famous research, the Seven Countries Study, and discovered the link between diet and heart disease. This study, which looked at the diets of men living in rural areas of Italy, Greece, Yugoslavia, Finland, the Netherlands, Japan, and the United States, clearly demonstrated that those subjects who consumed the most saturated fat had the highest blood-cholesterol levels and also the greatest incidence of heart attacks. Conversely, those who lived on the typical Mediterranean diet, based on olive oil, wine, whole grains (usually in the form of bread or pasta), vegetables, and fruit, were the healthiest and lived the longest. In short, Keys recognized the health benefits of the Mediterranean diet four decades before the Mediterranean Diet Pyramid (created by the Oldways Preservation & Exchange Trust and the Harvard School of Public Health) hit the American headlines in 1994. But even before this happened, heart-healthy olive oil had been getting some notice from the public. A new genre

of health-based cookbooks, starting with the 1959 publication of *Eat Well & Stay Well* (later reprinted with a subtitle, *The Mediterranean Way*) by Ancel and Mary Keys, gained ever-widening popularity, fueled in part by the natural-foods movement of the 1960s and 1970s.

The light began to dawn: not only was this traditional way of eating beneficial, but the food also tasted good. Before long, a new California gold rush was in the making. This time it was the green gold of good olive oil. New groves of olive trees were planted, and good olive oil was once again made and marketed.

THE VERSATILE OLIVE TREE

According to ancient Greek myth, the olive tree was a gift to mankind from Athena, goddess of wisdom. And what a gift it was. It provided oil for cooking and fuel for lamps, table olives, anointing

oil with mystical properties, medications, unguents, and cosmetics. To destroy an enemy's olive trees was considered sacrilege, and a display of utter ruthlessness.

To the Roman inheritors of the Greek world, olives and olive oil remained essential. In his celebrated second-century B.C. manual on farming, Cato the Elder devotes more space to making olive oil than anything else. Included in his list of necessary items for operating an olive farm of 240 iugera (one iugerum was about two-thirds of an acre) were assorted farming tools that are still familiar today, one ass for turning the mill, five "oil-pressing equipments" . . . and one hundred sheep.

The McEvoy Ranch staff passed on the ass-powered olive mill, but definitely endorse running sheep in the orchards. Then, as now, sheep graze on cover crops under the olive trees and simultaneously fertilize the soil. Furthermore, sheep can patter over wet ground that would stop a mowing machine in its tracks. Their only drawback is that once they've eaten the best grass, they start nibbling the bark off the trees. The herders counter this fatal habit (for the trees, not the sheep) by moving their woolly charges as often as twice a day, containing them within portable fencing. Soft bleating and tinkling neck bells announce their presence; it's a pretty sound. It is also a pretty sight, particularly when spring lambs are born in the orchards. They get a wonderful start in life on the lush green grass.

Cato exhorted olive farmers to be ever watchful and thrifty, and even gives directions for getting the best out of olive logs used for firewood. He recommended soaking the logs with *amurca*, the bitter, watery residue left after crushing olives for oil, and then drying the logs in the sun. "With this treatment," he notes, "they will not be smoky, but will burn well." Presumably this was waste wood; any worth saving would have been kept for carving into something useful. Dense and handsomely grained, but difficult to work because it is so hard and full of whorls, honey-colored olive wood has always been prized by craftsmen, who turn it into objects of intrinsic beauty to this day. In fact, this magical tree offers such a wealth of products it is small wonder that it has been cultivated—and revered—for thousands of years.

THE OLIVE ORCHARDS

Olive trees were probably first cultivated in areas of what are now Israel and Palestine in hot, dry conditions at least thirty-five hundred years ago

and gradually spread throughout the Mediterranean basin, reaching as far west as North Africa and Spain. Almost every Mediterranean culture lays claim to having invented olive oil, including the ancient Egyptians, who believed that the goddess Isis, consort of Osiris, introduced the olive tree, and the Greeks, who credited the goddess Athena. Archaeologists studying ancient Mediterranean civilizations continually find not only piles of discarded olive pits, but also clay storage jars and the remains of ancient olive mills and presses. With the European discovery of America in 1492, olive farming spread far beyond the Mediterranean basin; by 1560, olive groves were flourishing in Mexico.

The cultivated olive, *Olea europaea*, was bred from the wild oleaster, a straggly, thorny tree that bears a tiny fruit that is mostly pit. The wonder is that early man persevered at all with such an unlikely source of food. Olives contain a bitter glucoside that makes them inedible straight off the tree. It must be removed during the first stage of curing olives for the table, which can be done by soaking the fruit in brine, an alkaline solution, or even many changes of plain water. Much of this bitterness separates naturally with the watery component of the fruit when olives are pressed for their oil.

Hardy, broadleaf evergreens, olive trees are drought and heat tolerant, and will grow and produce even in poor soil, though of course they do a lot better with care. Once established, they can withstand a light frost, though not a sustained freeze, which would kill them back to the ground. If they suffer that fate, they will often regrow from the root crown.

Not surprisingly, olive trees thrive in California's Mediterranean climate. However, deciding to grow them organically for olive oil production in the semiarid hills of western Marin County presented a few difficulties. Summer heat does not bother the trees, but in order to produce a lot of fruit they need sufficient water. Also, many variations exist in the ranch soil: in some places it is formed from ancient serpentine rock high in magnesium, which olive trees abhor. In others, it is heavy clay, which had to be loosened and enriched.

Under the enlightened care of Tuscan agronomist and olive oil production consultant Maurizio Castelli, who flies in from Italy several times a year; orchard manager Shari DeJoseph; and Jeffrey Creque, the ranch's agricultural ecologist, the olive trees get plenty of attention, and today McEvoy Ranch is one of the few major olive oil producers in California to hold organic certification. Every precaution is taken to disturb the natural environment as little as possible, particularly the native oak and California bay woodlands that dominate the property. As Shari is quick to affirm, organic farming makes a better product for customers, and helps to protect the land and the olive trees. It also helps the local wildlife, which at McEvoy Ranch includes everything from badgers, deer, opossums, raccoons, skunks, wild turkeys, golden eagles, wild boar, jackrabbits, coyotes, snakes, and skinks to otters (the seasonal creek that runs through the property eventually joins up with the Petaluma River), and even bobcats and mountain lions. These big cats are rarely seen, but their tracks and kill are unmistakable.

In addition to providing water for the trees, the ranch's irrigation ponds provide a home for swans, and attract great blue herons, white egrets, and migrating waterfowl. The waters also teem with largemouth bass, catfish, crayfish, and trout.

Shari has had a lot of experience managing specialty crops and the propagation of seeds, which stands her in good stead at the ranch. She has the help of four full-time workers on a regular daily basis, but the number swells to well over fifty during harvest. An extensive drip-irrigation system supplied by annual runoff pumped from the ranch's ponds provides water directly to every tree, and cover crops like clover and vetch are planted in the orchards each fall to increase the soil's nitrogen and organic matter content, and to prevent erosion.

From late February through early May, a sheep rancher from nearby Tomales runs part of his flock in the orchards and, as previously noted, they help to fertilize the soil while cropping the grass. With this form of help, the trees—stressed by the sustained wet and cold of the long winter months—rebound quickly and are in optimum condition by the time they begin to bloom.

The cultivated olive is normally propagated clonally. Cuttings take readily in soil or by grafting, and are biologically identical to the parent tree. Shari propagates cuttings in large trays in the greenhouse. They start to produce roots in four to six weeks and are then transferred to individual containers. Depending on the variety and cultural techniques, olive trees begin bearing harvest-worthy fruit at three to four years, reach full maturity at eight to ten, and can continue producing fruit for literally centuries. In Europe, some gnarled survivors with massive trunks are reputed to be a thousand years old.

All varieties of olive trees are wind pollinated and many require fertilization from a different variety to produce fruit. For this reason, it is normal practice to mix olive varieties in an orchard, which can also add great depth of flavor to the finished oil. (Like some fine wines, most Tuscan-style oils are the result of expertly blended fruit.) Flower buds start appearing in April and are in full bloom by the end of May. Before they open, the buds look like minuscule olives, then turn into clusters of tiny, white blossoms that last for about two weeks. When they eventually drop, it looks as though a snow flurry had taken place.

The trees are cultivated in strict accordance with the United States Department of Agriculture's National Organic Program to maintain McEvoy's "certified organic" status. To help keep pests under control, bat houses have been installed in and around the orchards. Colonies of bats, who promptly set up housekeeping, come out at night to feed on insects, a task that is enthusiastically taken over by swallows, flycatchers, and other birds during the day. Great horned owls, Western screech owls, and barn owls all nest at the ranch, and swoop down on destructive little rodents that like to gnaw on the roots of the trees. It is natural preventative measures like these that help to keep the orchards healthy and the trees disease free.

To produce a California extra virgin olive oil in the Tuscan style with its characteristically rich, slightly peppery flavor, six Italian olive varieties are cultivated at McEvoy Ranch: Frantoio, Leccino, Pendolino, Maurino, Coratina, and Leccio del Corno. In addition, Kalamata and Sevillano olives are cultivated for making table olives for ranch use, although some oil varieties are also cured. A large collection of other varieties is also maintained for experimental purposes.

The first orchard was planted in 1992 on the highest hillside site, four hundred feet above sea level. The peak of the hill is well above the early morning fog that often obscures the ranch buildings in the valley below. Just a few palm trees poke up out of the fog bank, like so many ostriches trying to get a look at the surrounding circle of sunlit hills and Mount St. Helena far to the north. It's a stunning scene.

Following the harvest, which starts in mid-autumn, the olive trees rest but do not drop their leaves. In April, the first flower buds appear, and the age-old cycle starts again.

THE HARVEST

The olive harvest at McEvoy Ranch is the culmination of a year's hard work, and excitement runs high. It usually starts in late October or early November, and lasts for about four weeks. The time to start picking depends on the ripeness of the fruit. When the olives start to change from green to a variegated reddish purple, the race is on.

The actual commencement date is complicated by the fact that the various olive varieties do not all start to ripen at the same time, and different microclimates around the ranch also have to be taken into account. Shari endlessly inspects the trees. The grass beneath them is mowed and ground nets are

laid down to catch the picked fruit. Jeffrey, who supervises operation of the olive mill, works closely with journeyman oil maker José Chavez to make sure everything is ready for the production of olive oil. Maurizio flies in from Tuscany.

The process of making extra virgin olive oil is fairly simple. Unblemished fruit must be crushed immediately after picking, producing a pastelike mixture of oil, vegetation water (containing the bitter, water-soluble glucosides), seed fragments, and olive pulp. This paste or mash is then processed to separate the oil. In order for olive oil to be labeled "extra virgin," no chemical processes, or heat above 27 degrees Centigrade, can be utilized.

McEvoy extra virgin olive oil is made from a carefully balanced blend of olives, which are picked early to ensure the green, peppery style so typical of the best Tuscan oils. The fruit is grown, harvested, processed, and bottled at the ranch, making it true "estate-grown" oil. Early picking is crucial to the flavor, but of course half-ripe fruit yields far less oil. When judged ready to harvest, the olives are picked by a team of fifty or more workers, either by hand or by using pneumatic combs that clap the fruit off the trees. The fruit falls onto the nets and is immediately gathered into forty-pound lugs, which are then transferred to field bins and taken to the *frantoio*.

The state-of-the-art machinery in the McEvoy *frantoio* is made by the Rapanelli Company of Foligno, Italy, and includes the first and only installation of their proprietary Sinolea extractor in the United States, a unique percolation extraction system that gently separates the oil from the olive paste without heat or pressure.

After being washed, the olives are crushed by slowly revolving twin millstones of Italian granite that weigh over twelve hundred pounds each. The aromatic green paste that emerges is pumped to the Sinolea extractor, which is equipped with seven thousand steel blades that massage the paste and release the oil in tearlike drops into a trough below. Any vegetation water remaining in the oil is spun out by means of a centrifuge, and the oil is then ready for bottling as *olio nuovo*, "new oil," or is left to settle for general bottling, which takes place after a mellowing period of a few months. Following composting, the vegetation water and depleted olive paste (or pomace) is returned to the orchards to enrich the soil further. Nothing goes to waste.

The Sinolea oil extraction system stands in sharp contrast to the traditional method of placing the olive paste on woven straw mats, stacking them up, and exerting pressure via a screw press to squeeze out the oil and vegetation water, which are then separated from each other naturally by gravity or, in modern facilities, by centrifuge. (It is important to separate the oil from the vegetation water quickly, as this water will otherwise oxidize and damage the quality of the oil.) For thousands of years, such screw presses were turned by asses or donkeys walking in seemingly endless circles, and in some parts of the world, they still are.

Olio nuovo, the new oil made and sold during the olive harvest and for a few short weeks thereafter, is a luminescent product with the color and perfume of new-mown grass—the olive oil equivalent of Beaujolais nouveau. Robust, spicy, and fruity, its evanescent flavor and aroma are inimitable. By tradition, a small flask of *olio nuovo* is presented to every guest at the annual McEvoy Ranch Harvest Party. McEvoy friends and colleagues are invited to attend this spectacular event, which is held on two days in order to accommodate well over four hundred guests at a country buffet luncheon, complete with live music from several different musical groups. Wine flows and tables groan with an abundance of dishes that highlight produce from the ranch garden. With the harvest safely in, it is truly a time for thanksgiving and celebration.

EXTRA VIRGIN OLIVE OIL EXPLAINED

Four basic criteria for defining extra virgin olive oil have been set up by the International Olive Oil Council (IOOC), which is headquartered in Madrid, Spain. In brief, the oil must be extracted from olives that have not undergone any treatment other than washing, decantation, centrifugation, or filtration. It also must be "cold processed," must not exceed certain oleic acidity levels, and must have an aroma and flavor judged as worthy by a certified panel of official tasters.

Like noble wines or handmade cheeses, cold-processed extra virgin olive oils are labor-intensive to produce, and thus costly in the marketplace. But their superior quality expressed in aroma and flavor makes them worth their price. A premium, estate-grown olive oil is a fine condiment, to be savored and appreciated. Used as a dip for crusty bread, drizzled over vine-ripened tomatoes or a grilled steak, incorporated into a salad dressing, or stirred into a dish of white beans, a good olive oil can make all the flavor difference in the world. Many cooks like to reserve their best olive oil for

dipping bread and "finishing" dishes in this way, and utilize a less expensive olive oil for cooking. On the other hand, one can certainly cook with even the best of them. Although high heat will destroy the top flavor notes, it will still be apparent that a high-quality oil has been used. It is far more sensible to use up good olive oil quickly than to let it grow stale. Kept in the dark in a cool place, though not the refrigerator—never near the stove!—it will keep, unopened, for at least a year, and often much longer, from the date of bottling.

When shopping for olive oil, the American consumer is now faced with a bewildering choice of bottles from many different places in the world, among them Italy, France, Spain, Greece, Tunisia, Morocco, and, in recent years, California. As with wine, the flavor of olive oil depends on soil, climate, varieties of fruit, and the degree of ripeness at harvest. The ripeness of the fruit also affects color, which can range from dark green to sunny yellow. To complicate the issue further, it is perfectly legal for oil from, say, Tunisia to be shipped to France or Italy, bottled there, and sold in the United States as a French or Italian product. Prices vary wildly, from a few dollars to over fifty dollars for a half-liter bottle. But everyday table wines and fine vintages show a similar price range, and a bottle of olive oil goes a lot further than a bottle of wine.

Olive oil–producing countries typically make both premium extra virgin oils and inexpensive bulk oils. The latter are produced from lower-quality oils and olive pomace, rectified with chemical solvents that strip out high oleic acidity and undesirable aromas and flavors caused by problems such as defective fruit and poor manufacturing practices.

The process leaves the oils tasteless and odorless, and they are often blended with a little extra virgin olive oil for flavor before bottling. It is not uncommon for such oil to be falsely labeled as extra virgin and sold in the United States, which has no legal framework for regulating olive oil quality.

However, starting with the harvest of 2003, new regulations governing the labeling of oil for retail sale went into effect for all European Union member olive oil–producing countries. These require that a label for *extra virgin* oil state: "This is an olive oil of superior category produced directly from olives and only through mechanical processes." Furthermore, for an oil to be labeled as "first cold pressed," it must have been produced from the first pressing with a traditional hydraulic press at a temperature of less than 27 degrees Centigrade. The term "cold extraction" is reserved for oil produced at a similarly low temperature using a percolation (Sinolea) system or a centrifugal system (decanting centrifuge). Labels for plain olive oil or *pure olive oil,* composed of blends of refined olive oil and virgin oil, must state: "Oil containing exclusively olive oil which has undergone a refining process and oil produced directly from olives."

The IOOC actually has five classifications for olive oil, defined by varying oleic acidity levels and other characteristics: *extra virgin olive oil* must have a maximum oleic acidity level of 0.8 percent (down from 1 percent in previous years), *virgin olive oil* a maximum of 2 percent, *lampante olive oil* a maximum of 2 percent (down from 3.3 percent), *refined olive oil* a maximum of 0.3 percent (down from 0.5 percent), and plain *olive oil* no more than 1 percent (down from 1.5 percent). The low acidity levels of refined

and plain olive oils are achieved through the use of chemical solvents.

Incidentally, pale-colored "lite" olive oil is not an official grade recognized by the IOOC, but simply a marketing ploy for selling a virtually tasteless, chemically rectified olive oil that may or may not contain any virgin olive oil. It is not lower in calories or fat, and instead contains about 120 calories per tablespoon, just like any other vegetable oil.

In California, olive oil producers work hard to produce extra virgin olive oils that meet or exceed international standards, and can receive certification from the California Olive Oil Council (COOC), an

organization whose official tasting panel has been certified by the IOOC. There is nevertheless no *legal* criteria or enforcement of olive oil standards in the United States. The COOC certification is voluntary, yet remains the only consumer guarantee that a California olive oil does in fact meet internationally recognized standards for extra virgin olive oil.

LAVENDER AND HONEY

Along with serried ranks of young olive trees in pots, banks of aromatic lavender delight visitors as they arrive at McEvoy Ranch. A hardy perennial native to the Mediterranean basin, lavender is drought tolerant and does well in the local climate. There are over twenty-five species in the genus *Lavandula*, but only three varieties of lavender are cultivated at the ranch: *Lavandula x intermedia 'Grosso'*, a hybrid with silver-gray foliage, *L. x intermedia 'Provence'*, another hybrid with slate gray foliage (these two are cultivars of the same species, and both are good sources of lavender oil), and *L. angustifolia*, the true or English lavender. The last one, which is more delicate, is preferred for culinary use.

Lavender got its name from the Latin *lavare*, "to wash," as lavender was popularly used to scent rubbing oils used at the monumental public baths in ancient Rome. Its aroma is both soothing and uplifting, and it has been valued throughout the ages to scent linen, as an insect repellent, in medications, in cosmetics, and as a flavoring for foods. McEvoy-grown lavender is used to scent the ranch's hand-made olive oil soap, and its essential oil gives a wonderful fragrance to ranch-produced honey.

Honey, like olive oil, was highly prized in the ancient world, and was the most commonly used sweetener. It is produced by the common honeybee, *Apis mellifera*, from the nectar it finds in flowers. Depending on the floral source, the honey can be scented with acacia, clover, chestnut, orange, lavender, thyme, or any number of other flowers and herbs.

Starting about ten thousand years ago, Stone Age man gathered honey from the more-or-less bear-proof sites—usually hollows in tall trees or rocky cliffs—where wild bees made their nests, a practice known as bee hunting. By 2400 B.C., the Egyptians had discovered that bees could be induced to nest in horizontally stacked clay pipes instead of hollow trees, and they became beekeepers.

At Nan's request, Jeffrey introduced honeybee hives in the late 1990s, and he watches over the bees' continued welfare with the help of head gardener Margaret Koski-Kent and her crew. By way of encouragement, plants that specifically meet the bees' needs have been cultivated. The windy conditions that prevail at the ranch are less of a blessing to bees than to olives, which are wind pollinated, so the hives are located in sheltered spots.

Three or four main strains of *A. mellifera* are commonly found in California. At McEvoy Ranch, it was found that Caucasian bees were indolent and the Russian bees simply died, but the Italian strain tolerates the environment well, and the bees give an annual harvest of fifty to one hundred pounds of delicious millefleur honey per hive. After extraction and bottling, the honey is infused with McEvoy lavender, resulting in a honey with the

most wonderful aroma and flavor. It is used to great effect in the ranch kitchen, and is sold at the ranch shops to an eager audience—supplies are limited and quickly disappear.

THE KITCHEN GARDEN

The kitchen garden plays an important role in the day-to-day running of the ranch, and a strong emphasis is placed on cultivating heirloom vegetables and fruits.

Plant historians believe that the first five fruits to be brought in from the wild were olives, figs, dates, grapes, and pomegranates. Their earliest cultivation was in the so-called Fertile Crescent, which begins on the eastern shore of the Mediterranean Sea and curves around like a sickle moon to the Persian Gulf. All five appear in Egyptian tomb frescoes and are mentioned in the Bible and other ancient texts.

These five fruits all flourish at McEvoy Ranch today. Pomegranate and fig trees provide shade and fruit in the kitchen garden, a few of the palm trees around the main residence are date-bearing varieties, grapes are grown for the table, and, of course, thousands of olive trees are cultivated for oil and fruit.

All the fruits and vegetables in the fruit orchard and kitchen garden, the flowers for ranch events, the ornamentals that make up the landscaping—in fact, any plant that is not an olive tree—are the responsibility of Margaret and her crew of workers, part of whose job it is to provide the ranch kitchen with a year-round supply of seasonal produce. Plantings have to be carefully timed to ensure a continual supply. This bounty is used for everything from daily executive staff lunches and formal dinner parties for ranch guests to the annual harvest party. Any surplus fruits and vegetables are given to ranch workers to take home for their families, sold at the McEvoy Ranch shops, or offered at farmers' markets. Unusable material is composted.

Landscape designer Patrick Brennan created the original plan of the kitchen garden area, with its raised beds that outline the site, a supporting canopy for vines, and numerous trees and shrubs. The whole area is designed for walking and picking.

Margaret has overseen the care and management of these gardens since 1998. Driven by an enormous respect for organic diversity and the health of the soil, she plants for beauty, fragrance, visual interest, and usefulness. She has a marked preference for heirloom varieties and her seed list is extensive. She generally plants from her own seed bank, rather than purchasing seeds from large commercial companies, and she also buys new and unusual seed varieties from smaller companies who are equally committed to sustainable agriculture. Margaret relies on crop rotation, mulches, carefully chosen cover crops, and compost to maintain the fertility of the soil. All her methods are strictly organic, including putting in a blend of plants specifically to attract beneficial insects that prey on pests.

Delicate seedlings are transferred from the greenhouse to the soil early in the morning, when both the temperature and the soil are cool. Natural compost is all-important in Margaret's overall plan. She oversees the maintenance of large, rectangular, multilayered organic compost heaps, or "biscuits," that, when matured, are sifted to make the best possible planting material. All watering is carefully monitored and adjusted to the needs of each plant. Too little will stress plants. Too much can encourage luxuriant leaf growth at the expense of flavor and production.

As attractive as it is useful, the kitchen garden is a riot of color for much of the year. Flowering vines climb up the palm trees, and fantastically shaped gourds hang down from a leafy canopy. Black Mission figs with sweet pink flesh and delicate golden raspberries appear in their season, lemons and other citrus fruits proliferate, and root vegetables flourish in raised beds. The vegetable kingdom runs the gamut from amaranth and asparagus to zucchini. There are over twenty varieties of peppers and many different types of heirloom tomatoes. The bean family is represented by the Scarlet Runner, Painted Lady, Cherokee Trail of Tears, and Vernandon, a variety of *haricot vert*. Dozens of different kinds of lettuce flourish, and impressive stands of corn draw the eye upward. More delicate plants, such as *mâche* and pea shoots, are sheltered in glass frames.

Out in the fruit orchard, apple and pear trees share space with stone fruit trees such as apricots, peaches, and cherries. And at the very back of the kitchen garden, a large, shady hen run with nesting boxes contains a showy collection of poultry. These ornamental laying hens include beautifully plumaged Light and Buff Brahmas with feathered toes, fluffy bantam Blue Silkies, black-and-white Silver Penciled Wyandottes, White Rocks, golden Buff Orphingtons, and Black Astralorps and Auracanas. Highly sociable birds, they cluck and scratch about contentedly, are fed on organic grains,

and lay eggs in an extraordinary variety of sizes and colors that range from rich brown and pale green to ivory and pure white. In the kitchen, the problem of using eggs of such diverse size in recipes is dealt with by the tried-and-true expedient of *weighing* the freshly laid eggs. (A standard large egg weighs two ounces; two or three miniature Blue Silkie eggs might be needed to arrive at the same amount.)

Margaret feels that her horticultural work at the ranch has increased her respect and appreciation for the life cycles of individual plants; the cycles of the seasons; the whole integration of sun, moon, and earth on the land and its products; and the resultant life force that exhibits itself here in such profusion.

THE KITCHEN

The ranch kitchen is the domain that I share with my colleague, Mark Rohrmeier, and it is here that we plan—and execute—all ranch hospitality, from daily core staff lunches to major events like the annual harvest party. Designed on an open plan, the kitchen has a long butcher-block-topped island that separates the working area and appliances from a long polished American pine dining table surrounded by twelve high-backed Italian country chairs. Comfortably upholstered easy chairs at the end of the room, just inside the Dutch door, provide seating for visitors. On the walls are canvases by contemporary artists such as Wayne Thiebaud, Donald Roller Wilson, and Michael Taylor, part of Nan's extensive art collection. The room is filled with light from many oversized windows that offer views of the trees and courtyard outside, and even on a rainy winter day, it's a cheerful place.

The tale of how I arrived in this wonderful kitchen is a bit convoluted—and surprising, as I started my working life in the civil engineering department of the Southern Pacific Railroad Company! Suffice to say that the lure of the kitchen was too strong, and after graduating from the California Culinary Academy in San Francisco and working at a couple of small restaurants, I landed a job at Joyce Goldstein's great restaurant, Square One, where I began my love affair with olive oil. Some five years later, my wife and I decided to relocate our growing family to a rural area, and we moved to Sonoma County. There, I worked with Jan Birnbaum at his Catahoula Restaurant in Calistoga, where I learned the intricacies of wood-fired oven cookery, a skill that has since served me well at McEvoy Ranch.

After I was at the ranch for about a year, it became apparent that there was simply too much work for one chef to manage, and I was joined by the now indispensable Mark. He quickly became an integral part of ranch life, and has contributed several of the recipes in this book.

I feel strongly that even though the ranch is located out in the country, the food served here should meet cosmopolitan standards. I strive to make sure that all the elements of a dish are meaningful and not merely decorative, and both Mark and I are continually inspired by the glorious seasonal produce that flourishes—thanks to Margaret and her team—literally outside the kitchen door. Working with such great ingredients is both challenging and satisfying.

When cooking from this or any other book, I encourage you to taste, touch, smell, and feel the food you are preparing: to interact with it using all your senses. Only by doing this can you override the filter that these pages present between my kitchen and yours, and make my food into something else entirely: your food.

Soups, Salads, and Salad Dressings

Naturally enough, the ranch produce takes center stage when it comes to soups and salads. Margaret and her crew deliver a steady procession of different vegetables and fruits to the kitchen as they ripen. Some particular favorites, like the glorious heirloom tomatoes, are eagerly awaited with a crescendo of queries as to projected picking dates. I like to serve the tomatoes in a gazpacho (page 36) to start a summer lunch. On a blisteringly hot day, this same soup can be the whole meal, accompanied with crusty bread fresh from the brick oven and our own olive oil. In winter, on the other hand, a savory, filling bowl of Maurizio's Zuppa di Ceci (page 46) or of Mixed Winter Squash Soup (page 43), redolent with fresh sage and lavender honey, hits the spot.

The salads I have included in this chapter range from light to hearty—from a handful of fresh mixed greens with Red Wine Vinaigrette (page 66) to a hearty plate of Fresh Tuna Salad with Dry-Cured Black Olives (page 56). You will also find instructions for curing your own olives, a pair of salad dressings, and two rich and satisfying garnishes for soup, Aioli (page 69) and Rouille (page 70).

Lemon-Tarragon Gazpacho

SERVES 4 TO 6 *I like this soup best when made with perfect little Sun Gold cherry tomatoes, which carry extra sweetness, but it is delicious prepared with any peak-of-the-season heirloom tomatoes. Its sprightly flavor is most pronounced when freshly made, so try to serve the soup as soon as it is thoroughly chilled.*

2½ pounds vine-ripened heirloom tomatoes, cut into chunks if larger than cherry size

1 small red onion, about 3 ounces, cut into chunks

2 tablespoons firmly packed fresh tarragon leaves

Grated zest of 1 large lemon

2 teaspoons fresh lemon juice

¾ teaspoon sea salt or kosher salt

¼ teaspoon freshly ground pepper

Extra virgin olive oil for garnish

Chopped fresh tarragon for garnish

1. Working in batches, combine the tomatoes, onion, whole tarragon leaves, lemon zest and juice, salt, and pepper in a blender and process until smooth. Pass the purée through the fine screen of a food mill placed over a bowl. Taste and adjust the seasoning, cover, and refrigerate for at least 2 hours or for up to 12 hours.

2. Serve the soup in chilled bowls or teacups with a drizzle of extra virgin olive oil and a sprinkle of chopped tarragon.

Heirloom Tomato Soup

SERVES 6 TO 8 *Use only the most flavorful heirloom tomatoes to make this soup. Your patience in waiting until your local tomato season is at its peak will be repaid many times in the contents of your bowl. Also, cook the soup only until it simmers before puréeing, so that the flavor remains fresh. If you allow the tomatoes to boil for any length of time, the flavor will begin to resemble that of canned tomato soup.*

1 red onion, thinly sliced
2 tablespoons extra virgin olive oil
4 pounds vine-ripened heirloom tomatoes, cut into
   1-inch chunks
1 teaspoon sea salt or kosher salt
½ teaspoon freshly ground pepper
3 or 4 fresh basil leaves

1. In a heavy, 4-quart saucepan, combine the onion and olive oil over medium-low heat, cover, and sweat, stirring occasionally, until softened but not colored, about 10 minutes. Add the tomatoes, salt, and pepper, increase the heat to medium, cover partially, and cook, stirring occasionally, until the tomatoes have reached a simmer and are just softened.

2. Remove from the heat and let cool slightly. Working in batches, process the tomato mixture in a blender until smooth, adding 1 or 2 basil leaves to each. Pass the purée through the fine screen of a food mill placed over a clean saucepan. Reheat gently to serving temperature.

3. Taste and adjust the seasoning. Ladle the soup into warmed bowls and serve immediately.

Heirloom Tomato Gazpacho

SERVES 6 TO 8 *The quality of this soup depends on the quality of the tomatoes, so you must use tomatoes that taste great out of hand. Margaret grows many heirloom varieties for us. Each is subtly different, but they all share a great, larger-than-life flavor that is often sweeter and more acidic than commercial tomatoes, plus they tend to be juicier and more tender as well. A plant variety is not said to be heirloom until it is at least fifty years old. Many of these varieties have been out of commercial distribution at some point in their history, and have often been saved from extinction by dedicated gardeners and small farmers who value them for their taste over their suitability to mass production and long-distance transport. Farmers' markets, specialty stores, and local farmers are all good local sources for heirlooms. The amount of habanero chile will make a medium-spicy soup. You can adjust the heat level to taste.*

3 ½ pounds vine-ripened heirloom tomatoes, cut into chunks

1 unpeeled Armenian, English, or Japanese cucumber, cut into chunks

1 red onion, cut into chunks

½ habanero chile, stem, seeds, and ribs removed

2 large cloves garlic, cut in half

2 tablespoons sherry vinegar

¼ cup extra virgin olive oil

½ teaspoon sea salt or kosher salt

½ teaspoon freshly ground pepper

Extra virgin olive oil or plain yogurt for garnish

Chopped fresh mint for garnish

1. In a nonreactive container, combine the tomatoes, cucumber, onion, chile, garlic, vinegar, olive oil, salt, and pepper. Cover and refrigerate for at least 12 hours or up to 36 hours, stirring once or twice.

2. Working in batches, process the tomato mixture in a blender until smooth. Pass the purée through the fine screen of a food mill placed over a bowl. Taste and adjust the seasoning. Serve immediately in chilled bowls with a drizzle of olive oil or yogurt and a sprinkle of mint.

Mussel Soup with Swiss Chard, Tomato, and Aioli

SERVES 4 TO 6 *I love this combination of flavors: the briny flavor of the mussels makes a wonderful counterpoint to the tomatoes, chard, and garlic. When cutting garlic, you may notice a green sprout inside. This is the start of a new garlic plant, and it begins forming when garlic has been in storage for any length of time. Always remove and discard this sprout, as it has a strong, unpleasant flavor.*

4 large cloves garlic

3 slices country-style bread, each about 7 inches long by 4 inches wide by ½ inch thick

1½ teaspoons plus ¼ cup extra virgin olive oil

1 large yellow onion, chopped

2 pounds plum tomatoes, peeled, seeded, and cut into ¼-inch-wide strips, or 1 can (28 ounces) Italian plum tomatoes, drained and chopped

4 cups Fish Fumet (page 108) or reconstituted frozen fish stock

¾ teaspoon sea salt or kosher salt

½ teaspoon freshly ground pepper

1 bunch Swiss chard, about 1 pound, tough stems removed and leaves cut crosswise into ½-inch-wide ribbons

1½ cups dry white wine

2½ pounds mussels, scrubbed and debearded

Aioli (page 69) for serving

1. Cut 1 garlic clove in half and evenly slice the remaining 3 cloves; set aside. Brush the bread slices on both sides with the 1½ teaspoons olive oil. Grill or toast until golden brown on both sides, then rub with the cut sides of the halved garlic clove. Cut each slice into 4 triangles.

2. In a large, heavy pot, heat the ¼ cup olive oil over medium-low heat. Add the onion and sliced garlic and cook, stirring occasionally, until the onion is sweet and tender, about 10 minutes. Add the tomatoes, fumet, salt, and pepper. Increase the heat and bring the mixture to a simmer. Reduce the heat and simmer for 10 minutes to blend the flavors. Add the chard and simmer for 3 to 4 minutes.

3. While the chard is cooking, bring the wine to a boil in a large sauté pan over high heat. Add the mussels, cover, and cook until the mussels open, 3 to 4 minutes. Using tongs or a slotted spoon, remove the mussels from the sauté pan and the chard from the broth and divide among individual bowls. If some mussels have not opened, you can

continued

cook them for another minute or two. If they still fail to open, discard them. Strain the mussel cooking liquid through a fine-mesh sieve into the hot broth. Taste and adjust the seasoning.

4. Ladle the broth over the mussels and chard, dividing it evenly, and garnish with the bread triangles. Top each serving with a generous drizzle of Aioli.

VARIATION: *With a few small changes, this soup can be made into a wonderful pasta dish. Cook your chosen pasta (I like spaghetti or linguine with this sauce) until almost done, drain, and toss with 1 tablespoon olive oil to prevent sticking. In the recipe, omit the fumet and reduce the white wine to 1/2 cup. Add the 1/2 cup wine and a generous pinch of red pepper flakes (optional) to the onion along with the tomatoes, salt, and pepper and bring the mixture to a boil over high heat. Add the mussels, cover, and cook for 2 minutes, shaking the pan occasionally. Add the chard and the drained pasta, and continue cooking for another 2 minutes. Discard any mussels that have not opened, and add 1/4 cup (or more) full-flavored extra virgin olive oil. Taste and adjust the seasoning, and serve at once.*

How to Make a Puréed Vegetable Soup

Puréed vegetable soups are easy to make. In general, begin by slowly cooking 1 large yellow onion, chopped, in a few tablespoons olive oil over medium-low heat until soft but not colored, 5 to 10 minutes. Next, add some salt, your vegetable of choice, and some liquid, which can be vegetable stock, chicken stock, or water. Increase the heat to high, bring the liquid to a boil, reduce the heat to a simmer, and cook until the vegetable is tender. Then either purée the soup in a stand blender or use an immersion blender (sometimes known as a stick blender), which allows you to purée the soup directly in the pan. Pass the soup through the fine screen of a food mill to remove any fibrous bits that were not completely puréed. Finally, adjust the seasoning and consistency as necessary.

Slow-cooked onion develops a mellow flavor and adds body and sweetness to the soup without imparting a strong taste or affecting the color. In the case of darker soups with more complex flavors such as mushroom or onion, cook the onion longer, until it starts to caramelize, to add a richer, deeper taste.

If you are using green vegetables such as peas and spinach, add the liquid and salt first and bring the liquid to a full boil before adding the vegetable. This ensures that the color of the vegetable will remain bright. Keep the soup at a full boil, rather than reduce the heat, and cook only until the vegetable is tender before puréeing. You can improve the consistency of spinach, sorrel, or other soups made with delicate greens by cooking a peeled and thinly sliced russet potato in the liquid before adding the green vegetable.

Starchy vegetables such as potatoes, carrots, winter squashes, and dried legumes require proportionally more liquid than moisture-rich vegetables such as spinach (which requires very little) and tomato (which requires none). Most vegetables fall in between, and adding enough liquid just to cover them usually results in a good consistency.

Mixed Winter Squash Soup with Honey and Sage

SERVES 6 TO 8 *This is one of Mark's great recipes. The three varieties of squash reinforce one another to produce a fuller flavor. Feel free to use fewer varieties or to substitute others. There is great variation in starchiness in squashes, both by age and type. In some cases, you might have to thin this soup quite a bit to achieve the desired consistency. I judge the consistency by dipping a little soup out of the pot with a spoon and then letting it pour back in. If the surface briefly holds a slight mound where the soup fell, the consistency is correct.*

1 kabocha squash, about 2 pounds

1 Red Kuri squash, about 2 pounds

1 butternut squash, about 2 pounds

4 tablespoons extra virgin olive oil

Sea salt or kosher salt

Freshly ground white pepper

1 cup chopped yellow onion

4 cups vegetable or chicken stock, plus extra for thinning if needed

2 tablespoons chopped fresh sage

2 tablespoons honey

1. Preheat the oven to 300°F. Rub the 3 whole squashes with 1 tablespoon of the olive oil and sprinkle with salt and pepper. Place them on a rimmed baking sheet and roast in the oven, turning once or twice, until they are tender when pierced with a knife and browned, 1½ to 2 hours. Remove the squashes from the oven and let stand until cool enough to handle. Halve, seed, peel, and chop the squashes. Measure 8 cups chopped squash; reserve the remainder in the refrigerator for another use.

2. In a saucepan, heat 2 tablespoons of the olive oil over low heat. Add the onion and cook, stirring occasionally, until sweet and tender, about 10 minutes. Add the chopped squash and 4 cups stock, and bring to a boil over high heat, stirring frequently. Reduce the heat to low and simmer, uncovered, until the squash is very soft, about 10 minutes.

3. Remove from the heat and let cool slightly. Working in batches, process the squash mixture in a blender until smooth and transfer to a clean pot. Reheat gently to serving temperature, and add the sage, honey, and the remaining 1 tablespoon olive oil. Thin with additional broth or water if necessary to achieve the proper consistency.

4. Season to taste with salt and pepper. Ladle into warmed bowls and serve immediately.

Fish Soup with Asparagus and Spring Garlic

SERVES 6 *Use several kinds of firm-fleshed white fish for the best flavor. Spring garlic is the immature garlic plant, harvested when it is less than an inch in diameter and before a bulb has formed at the base. The plants resemble leeks and should be cooked in the same way. They add a relatively mild garlic flavor to dishes, and make a flavorful addition to soups, stews, and mixed sautéed vegetables. If spring has passed or you can't find spring garlic, substitute a second leek and a thinly sliced clove of garlic. Serve the soup with a loaf of crusty bread and a nice bottle of wine—the same wine you used in the soup.*

1 large leek, white and light green parts only, split lengthwise and sliced crosswise ⅛ inch thick

1 large yellow onion, diced

1 pound spring garlic, white and light green parts only, split lengthwise and sliced crosswise ⅛ inch thick

¼ cup extra virgin olive oil

1 teaspoon sea salt or kosher salt

1½ cups fruity, dry white wine such as a Sauvignon Blanc or an un-oaked Chardonnay, boiled to reduce to ¾ cup

2 quarts Fish Fumet (page 108) or reconstituted frozen fish stock

1½ pounds assorted firm white fish fillets, cut into 1-inch chunks

1 pound asparagus, tough ends removed and cut on the diagonal into slices ⅛ inch thick

6 tablespoons extra virgin olive oil for serving

1. In a large, heavy pot, combine the leek, onion, garlic, olive oil, and salt over medium-low heat. Cover and sweat the vegetables, stirring occasionally, until softened but not colored, 15 to 20 minutes.

2. Increase the heat to medium-high, add the reduced wine and the fumet, and bring to a boil. Add the fish, reduce the heat to low, and simmer for 3 minutes. Add the asparagus and continue simmering until the fish is opaque throughout and the asparagus is tender, about 3 minutes longer. Taste and adjust the seasoning.

3. Ladle the soup into warmed bowls. Drizzle 1 tablespoon olive oil on top of each bowl and serve immediately.

Puréed Artichoke Soup

SERVES 6 TO 8 *This soup is best in the spring when artichokes are young, tender, and mild and have not yet developed a fuzzy choke. It can, however, be made anytime that you have fresh artichokes. Just select the freshest specimens available of any size. For a more substantial meal, sauté seasoned cubes of chicken breast in olive oil and add to the soup just before serving.*

1 yellow onion, thinly sliced

2 tablespoons extra virgin olive oil

1 small russet potato, about 3 ounces, peeled and cut into chunks

1 celery stalk, cut into chunks

3 cups water

Sea salt or kosher salt

Juice of 1 lemon

1½ pounds baby artichokes

Freshly grated Parmigiano-Reggiano cheese for serving

Freshly ground pepper for serving

Extra virgin olive oil for serving

1. In a heavy, 4-quart saucepan, combine the onion and olive oil over medium-low heat. Cover and sweat, stirring occasionally, until the onion is softened but not colored, about 10 minutes. Add the potato, celery, water, and ³/₄ teaspoon salt and bring to a boil.

2. Meanwhile, prepare the artichokes. Put a large pot of water on to boil (at least 4 quarts). Fill a bowl with water and add the lemon juice. Trim one-third off the top of each artichoke, then trim off the darkened stem end. Snap off the outer leaves until you reach the tender, yellow-green inner leaves. Trim off any dark green parts remaining around the base. Cut each artichoke in half lengthwise if they are small; if they are larger, cut into 6 or 8 wedges. If there is a fuzzy choke, use a small spoon or sharp-tipped paring knife to remove it. To retard browning, drop the pieces into the bowl of lemon water. When the pot of water reaches a full boil, add 2 tablespoons salt for each 4 quarts water. When the water returns to a full boil, drain the artichokes, add them to the boiling water, and cook until they are almost tender, about 4 minutes. Drain the artichokes and add them to the boiling soup base.

3. Reduce the heat to a simmer and continue cooking until all the vegetables are tender, 5 to 10 minutes. Remove from the heat and let cool slightly. Working in batches, process the artichoke mixture in a blender until smooth. Pass the purée through the fine screen of a food mill placed over a clean saucepan. Reheat gently to serving temperature. Thin with additional water if necessary to achieve proper consistency. Taste and adjust the seasoning.

4. Ladle the soup into warmed bowls. Top each bowl with some cheese, a sprinkle of pepper, and a drizzle of your best olive oil.

Maurizio's Zuppa di Ceci

SERVES 4 TO 6 *Ceci is the Italian word for chickpeas or garbanzo beans. This is Maurizio Castelli's version of a classic Tuscan soup. On a rainy winter day, ladle some into a bowl, add homemade croutons, and drizzle with extra virgin olive oil. We like to serve it with our freshly made olio nuovo. The flavor is simple but hearty, with the beans and sage providing a nice base for the vigorous blast of the new harvest oil. The croutons will keep well for a few days in a tightly covered container, so make extra if you like them. Thin slices of baguette can also be made into croutons in a similar manner: Using a small pastry brush, apply a very thin coat of oil to both sides of the slices and arrange them in a single layer on the baking sheet. Watch them carefully and turn them over once they begin to brown. Return them to the oven to brown the other side, which will happen very quickly.*

2 cups dried chickpeas

1½ quarts water

½ yellow onion, cut into chunks

1 celery stalk, cut into chunks

1 large carrot, peeled and cut into ½-inch-thick slices

2 cloves garlic, peeled

2 tablespoons extra virgin olive oil

6 fresh sage leaves

croutons

2 slices country-style bread, each about 7 inches long by 4 inches wide by ⅜ inch thick

1 tablespoon extra virgin olive oil

Pinch of sea salt or kosher salt

Pinch of freshly ground pepper

¾ teaspoon sea salt or kosher salt

Extra virgin olive oil for serving

1. The day before serving, pick over the chickpeas and remove any dirt or stones. Rinse the chickpeas, place them in a 2-quart container, and add the water. Cover the container and refrigerate overnight.

2. The next day, in a heavy, 2- or 3-quart saucepan, combine the onion, celery, carrot, garlic, and 2 tablespoons of the olive oil over medium-low heat. Cover and sweat the vegetables, stirring occasionally, until softened but not colored, about 10 minutes. Add the chickpeas and their soaking liquid, increase the heat to high, and bring to a boil. Reduce the heat to a gentle boil, add the sage leaves, cover partially, and cook until the chickpeas are very tender, about 2 hours. Stir them occasionally, and add more water as necessary to keep them covered by about 1 inch.

3. While the chickpeas are cooking, prepare the croutons: Preheat the oven to 325°F. Lay the bread slices on top of each other on a work surface. Using a sharp knife, cut off the crusts and discard. Cut the slices into 3/8-inch-wide strips, and then cut the strips, at right angles, into 3/8-inch cubes. Place the cubes in a small bowl and toss well with the olive oil, salt, and pepper. Transfer to a rimmed baking sheet and place in the oven. Bake, stirring every 2 minutes, until golden brown, about 6 minutes. Breads brown at different rates, so watch the cubes carefully.

4. When the chickpeas are tender, remove the soup from the heat, let cool slightly, add the salt, and pass the contents of the pan through the medium screen of a food mill placed over a clean saucepan. You may blend the soup first for a smoother texture, but you should still pass it through the food mill to remove the bits of tough skin that remain in the soup. Reheat gently to serving temperature. Thin with additional water if necessary to achieve the proper consistency.

5. Taste and adjust the seasoning. Ladle the soup into warmed bowls and top with a drizzle of olive oil and some of the homemade croutons.

Fava Bean, Artichoke, and Olive Salad

SERVES 6 *Every fall, Margaret plants fava beans in the kitchen garden, where they perform many valuable tasks. Their deep roots break up the soil far below the surface, and bacteria-containing nodules on these roots "fix" nitrogen in the soil by changing it into a form that plants can use. Their leafy tops disperse heavy rainfall and help to prevent the soil from washing away. Their black and white flowers attract beneficial insects and, as a bonus, are quite beautiful. Most importantly the wonderful beans these plants produce are, in our part of the world, one of the earliest harbingers of spring. Finally, when the spent fava bean plants are composted, all their nutrients and organic matter are returned to the soil, increasing its tilth.*

Young fava beans are good by themselves, but I think they truly shine in combination with other vegetables. Some particularly complementary companions are artichokes, onions, peas, asparagus, and mushrooms, especially chanterelles. (If you have a garden, try growing some favas at home. Plant the seeds 2 inches deep in early fall before the frost. The plants will germinate with the rains and grow larger as the temperatures moderate in the spring.) In this salad, fava beans are combined with baby artichokes and briny olives in a light lemon vinaigrette: a perfect beginning to a spring meal.

vinaigrette

½ cup extra virgin olive oil

2 ½ tablespoons fresh lemon juice, preferably
  Meyer lemon

1 tablespoon red wine vinegar

2 tablespoons finely chopped shallot

½ teaspoon sea salt or kosher salt

½ teaspoon freshly ground pepper

2 pounds young fava beans

Juice of 1 lemon

12 baby artichokes

1 tablespoon extra virgin olive oil

2 cloves garlic

1 bay leaf

Sea salt or kosher salt

12 Kalamata or home-cured olives (page 58),
  pitted and coarsely chopped

3 tablespoons finely julienned fresh mint leaves

½ pound (6 to 8 cups) mixed baby lettuce leaves or
  torn lettuce

Small wedge of Parmigiano-Reggiano cheese (optional)

continued

1. To prepare the vinaigrette, in a small bowl, whisk together all the ingredients. Taste and adjust the seasoning.

2. Shell the fava beans. Peel the outer skin from 1 bean to see if the bean is tender and sweet enough to serve raw. If it is, remove the skin from each bean using the tip of your fingernail or a small knife. If not, blanch the beans in salted, boiling water for 45 to 60 seconds, drain, immerse in a bowl of cold water, and slip off the skins. Set the fava beans aside.

3. Fill a bowl with water and add the lemon juice. Trim one-third off the top of each artichoke, then trim off the darkened stem end. Snap off the outer leaves until you reach the tender, yellow-green inner leaves. Trim off any dark green parts remaining around the base. Cut each artichoke in half lengthwise. If there is a fuzzy choke, use a small spoon or sharp-tipped paring knife to remove it. To retard browning, drop the artichoke halves into the lemon water. When all the artichokes have been trimmed, drain the artichokes and place them in a shallow saucepan with the olive oil, garlic, bay leaf, $1/4$ teaspoon salt, and a few tablespoons of water. Bring to a simmer over medium heat, cover partially, and braise until just tender, stirring occasionally, about 7 minutes. Drain and let cool to room temperature. Taste and adjust the seasoning.

4. In a bowl, combine the artichokes, fava beans, olives, and mint with about half of the vinaigrette, and toss to coat evenly.

5. Place the greens in a large bowl and season with a few grains of salt. Drizzle with enough of the remaining vinaigrette to coat lightly, and toss well. Arrange the greens on chilled salad plates. Spoon the fava mixture evenly over the greens. For a slightly richer presentation, shave a few thin slices of Parmigiano-Reggiano cheese over the top of each salad.

VARIATION: *This salad is also good made with raw artichokes. You need fresh, crisp artichokes (the larger sizes are fine) and a very sharp knife. Artichokes discolor when cut, so as close as possible to serving time, prepare the artichokes as directed and drop them into ice water to which the juice of 1 lemon has been added until ready to use. Toss the fava beans, olives, and mint as directed. Remove the artichokes from the lemon water, pat them dry, slice them as quickly and as thinly as possible, put them into the bowl with the favas, and toss to coat. Proceed as directed.*

Herbed Cherry Tomato Salad

SERVES 4 *Here is the perfect accompaniment to classic dishes from India. By changing the herbs, it can also complement other cuisines. For instance, if you substitute flat-leaf parsley for the cilantro and mint, it goes well with Italian dishes. For Greek dishes, replace the cilantro with dill or oregano. To give the salad a southern French flavor, use tarragon in place of the cilantro and mint.*

2 cups cherry tomatoes, stemmed and cut in half

1 cup mixed fresh herbs such as cilantro leaves, julienned regular and/or purple basil, and julienned mint leaves

1 tablespoon extra virgin olive oil

2 teaspoons fresh lemon juice

½ teaspoon sea salt or kosher salt

¼ teaspoon freshly ground pepper

In a bowl, combine all the ingredients and toss to combine, then serve.

Triticale Salad with Sun-Dried Tomato Vinaigrette

SERVES 6 *Triticale, a hybrid grain, is the result of a cross between wheat and rye. Either of these would be a good substitute in this salad. Another alternative is* farro, *an ancient variety of wheat that is a Tuscan favorite. Look for it in Italian delicatessens and natural-foods stores. Whole grains make this salad filling and satisfying. Changing the grain used will also change the cooking time. Check the doneness periodically, starting after 30 minutes.*

1 cup triticale

6 cups water

1 teaspoon sea salt or kosher salt

vinaigrette

1½ tablespoons diced oil-packed sun-dried tomato

1 shallot, finely chopped

¼ cup extra virgin olive oil

1 tablespoon walnut oil

2 tablespoons red wine vinegar

1 teaspoon balsamic vinegar

½ teaspoon sea salt or kosher salt

¼ teaspoon freshly ground pepper

3 tablespoons chopped walnuts, lightly toasted

2 tablespoons chopped fresh flat-leaf parsley

1. In a saucepan, combine the triticale and water and bring to a simmer over medium heat. Adjust the heat to maintain a simmer and cook, uncovered, adding more water if necessary to keep the grains submerged, until the grain is tender but still chewy, about 1 hour. Season with the salt during the last 15 minutes of cooking. Drain in a colander and rinse briefly under running cold water. Drain again and allow to cool in the colander.

2. Meanwhile, prepare the vinaigrette: In a small bowl, whisk together all the ingredients. Taste and adjust the seasoning.

3. In a bowl, combine the cooled triticale and the vinaigrette and toss to coat evenly. Add the walnuts and parsley and toss again. If time permits, allow the salad to stand at room temperature for an hour or two before serving to blend the flavors. Taste and adjust the seasoning just before serving.

Warm Goat Cheese Salad with Lavender Honey

SERVES 6 *Laura Chenel started the American goat cheese, or chèvre, craze after making a trip to France in the late 1970s. Her dairy is located just east of the town of Sonoma, and today her wonderful cheeses are shipped all over the United States. I like to combine her mild, creamy goat cheese with the aromatic floral notes of our lavender honey. I coat rounds of the cheese with a lavender-scented walnut crust and warm them in the oven. I then put the cheese together with some fruit, bread, and a small salad, producing a variety of tastes, textures, and temperatures—warm, cool, salty, sweet, acid, creamy, crunchy—all on one plate.*

½ cup dry country-style bread chunks

¼ cup walnut pieces, lightly toasted

½ teaspoon fresh lavender flowers
 (*Lavandula angustifolia*)

¼ teaspoon freshly ground pepper

6 rounds mild fresh goat cheese, each about
 2 ounces and 1 inch thick

6 small handfuls (about 3 ounces) mixed baby
 lettuce leaves

¼ cup Red Wine Vinaigrette (page 66)

18 thin slices baguette, baked with walnuts
 if available

1 small bunch seedless grapes, or 1 large nectarine,
 pitted and sliced lengthwise

3 tablespoons lavender honey

1. Preheat the oven to 375°F. Line a baking sheet with baking parchment. In a food processor, combine the dry bread, walnuts, lavender flowers, and pepper and pulse until the crumbs are the consistency of coarse sand. Pour out onto a plate. Roll the cheese rounds in the crumbs, patting with your hands to help the crumbs adhere to the cheese. Place the coated cheese rounds on the prepared baking sheet. Bake the cheese rounds until lightly golden, 10 to 12 minutes.

2. While the cheese is baking, place the lettuce in a bowl, drizzle with the vinaigrette, and toss to coat the leaves evenly.

3. Remove the cheese from the oven and, using a spatula, transfer to salad plates. Garnish each plate with 3 baguette slices, some grapes or nectarine slices, and an equal amount of the dressed lettuce. Drizzle each cheese round with 1½ teaspoons of the honey. Serve immediately.

Fresh Tuna Salad with Dry-Cured Black Olives

MAKES 2 CUPS; SERVES 4 AS A LIGHT MEAL *This combination makes an exceptional salad, and is equally good as a filling for halved avocados, or in sandwiches. I use tombo tuna, also known as albacore, for this salad, but any fresh tuna will do.*

1 tuna steak, about ¾ pound and 1 inch thick

1 tablespoon fennel seeds, lightly toasted in a dry pan

1 tablespoon peppercorns

About 1 cup extra virgin olive oil

1 red onion, finely diced

2 celery stalks, with some leaves, finely diced

2 tablespoons salt-packed capers, soaked in warm
    water for 10 minutes, drained, and chopped

⅓ cup dry-cured black olives, pitted and chopped

dressing

1 clove garlic, chopped

2 anchovy fillets, preferably salt packed, rinsed
    and chopped

Rounded ¼ teaspoon sea salt or kosher salt

½ teaspoon freshly ground pepper

1 egg yolk

Reserved olive oil, plus extra if needed

Fresh lemon juice

1. Select a saucepan just large enough to hold the tuna steak. Place the fennel seeds and peppercorns in a square of cheesecloth, bring together the corners, and tie securely, or place the spices in a tea ball. Add to the tuna along with the olive oil just to cover. Place over very low heat and cook very slowly, turning once halfway through the cooking, until the tuna is nearly cooked through, about 15 minutes. Remove from the heat and lift the tuna from the oil. Place the tuna in the refrigerator for 10 minutes to stop the cooking. Reserve the oil.

2. When the tuna is cool, break it into rough chunks and place in a bowl. Add the onion, celery, capers, and olives.

3. To prepare the dressing, in a small bowl, combine the garlic, anchovies, salt, and pepper, and mash together with a fork. Add the egg yolk and mix well. Whisk in the reserved olive oil in a slow, thin stream, as you would when making a mayonnaise. Add a little more oil if necessary to make a fairly thick sauce. Season to taste with lemon juice, then adjust with more salt and pepper.

4. Add the dressing to the tuna and vegetable mixture and stir to blend. Check the seasoning again, then serve.

Home-Cured Olives

Most Americans have grown up with the canned ripe black olives that are the mainstay of the California olive industry. These olives are cured quickly in an aerated lye solution that both removes the bitter glucosides and turns the fruits a uniform black. The color is set further by the addition of a small amount of ferrous gluconate. The resulting olives are even in color and texture, but insipid in flavor. This is in contrast to the very flavorful olives that are made in Mediterranean countries by a variety of slower methods, most of which involve gradual leaching of the glucosides from the olives in water or salt brine. The process can be as simple as packing the olives in a mesh bag and submerging the bag in the ocean or a stream until the flavor is acceptable. More commonly, olives are put into a salt brine that is changed periodically until the glucosides have been leached. Another method calls for burying large, ripe olives in coarse salt and letting the salt draw the glucosides and much of the moisture from the fruit. These are known as dry-cured olives, and they are wonderfully meaty and chewy with a salty tang.

We have developed the following method for curing olives grown at the ranch. This method can be used for all varieties of olives and various degrees of ripeness, as long as the fruit is sound and unblemished. Raw olives are sturdy-looking things, but they are actually fragile, with thin skins that are easily punctured. The flesh, although firm, bruises readily and begins to ferment rapidly from microorganisms introduced through punctures and soft spots. We cure fruit at all stages of ripeness and find merit in all the varieties and degrees of ripeness that we have tried. Some of our particular favorites are ripe Kalamata, half-ripe Pendolino and Frantoio, and both green and ripe Sevillano.

Once you have the olives, you will need only water, Mason jars with lids (use the lids with red sealant as the gray sealant used on some lids will not stand up to the oil used later in the process), sea salt, and red wine vinegar. First, rinse the olives well in water and place them in sterilized Mason jars. Fill the jars to the brim with water and screw on the lids just snug. Place the jars on a tray to catch any overflow and put them in a cool, dark place. Leave them undisturbed for 1 week. They may appear to be carbonated, with small bubbles visible on the surface of the olives. This is a natural fermentation that will enhance the flavor of the olives. Carefully remove the lids from the jars and drain off the water. For sanitary reasons, it is important not to touch the olives or to touch anything, such as the bowl of a spoon, with which they might come into contact. Refill the jars with clean water, replace their lids, and leave in a cool, dark place for another week.

Drain off the water from the jars as before and refill them with brine made by dissolving 1 cup sea salt in 4 quarts water. You need not be concerned about making an exact quantity of brine because you will be changing it weekly for the next few months and any excess brine can be stored in a nonreactive container. Drain the jars and refill them with fresh brine each week. After about 6 weeks, use a clean spoon to remove a representative olive before changing the brine. Taste a small piece to assess how the curing is progressing. If the olive is still too bitter, change the brine, wait another week, and try again. It is difficult to predict how long this process will take. The variety of olives, their ripeness, and ambient temperature all affect the process, which can last from 6 weeks to 15 weeks—or even more. Remember, the model is not the California ripe olive, but one of the more flavorful imported olives.

When a taste of a few representative olives from a batch indicates that enough of the bitterness has leached away, drain off the curing brine one final time and refill with a storage brine made by dissolving 2/3 cup sea salt in 4 quarts water and 3 cups red wine vinegar. Pour enough olive oil onto the surface of the liquid in each jar to form a layer 1/8 inch deep, and replace the lids. It is best to store the unopened jars in the refrigerator, although a cool, dark place is acceptable. When you open a jar, remember to use a clean utensil, never your fingers, to remove the olives. Once a jar is open, store it in the refrigerator and use within 1 month.

Apple Wood-Smoked Salmon Salad with Pickled Onions and Apples

SERVES 6 TO 8 *I created this recipe for the wedding of a former coworker, Eliza Fischer, which took place at the Apple Farm in Mendocino County's Anderson Valley. Eliza and her fiancé, David, wanted a recipe to give to their guests along with a bundle of apple-wood twigs from the trees at the farm. I decided to hot-smoke local king salmon using these twigs. Freshly cooked smoked salmon is worlds away from the dense product with which you are probably familiar. It is moist and tender and has the added punch of an intense smoky flavor. At the ranch, we use apple-wood twigs saved from the annual orchard pruning, but apple-wood chips packaged for barbecue use also work well. If apple wood is unavailable, other fruit woods can be used, but stay away from hardwoods, which have too strong a flavor. Use fresh wild salmon, rather than farm raised, if you can. It is also worthwhile to search out a good cider vinegar. Some of the nationally distributed brands are actually only cider-flavored vinegar. The onion and apple pickles may be prepared the day before.*

pickles

2 quarts plus ¾ cup water

1 red onion, sliced ⅛ inch thick and separated
into rings

1 large, tart, crisp apple such as Granny Smith,
unpeeled, halved, cored, and sliced ⅛ inch thick

¾ cup cider vinegar

¼ cup thawed, frozen apple juice concentrate

4 juniper berries, bruised

1 small piece cinnamon stick, about 2 inches long

salmon

1 side salmon with skin intact, 2 to 3 pounds, scaled
and pin bones removed

1 teaspoon sea salt or kosher salt

1 teaspoon freshly ground pepper

¼ teaspoon ground cinnamon

¼ teaspoon ground allspice

1 small bundle apple-wood twigs or 1 cup apple-wood
wood chips, soaked overnight in water

1 tablespoon thawed, frozen apple juice concentrate

vinaigrette

¼ cup extra virgin olive oil

2 tablespoons cider vinegar

1 tablespoon thawed, frozen apple juice concentrate

¼ teaspoon sea salt or kosher salt

¼ teaspoon freshly ground pepper

⅛ teaspoon ground cinnamon

2 heads romaine or other crisp lettuce, leaves
separated and torn into bite-sized pieces (about
2½ quarts)

2 celery stalks, thinly sliced

Sea salt or kosher salt

Freshly ground pepper

continued

1. To prepare the pickles, pour the 2 quarts water into a saucepan and bring to a boil over high heat. Add the onion rings, then immediately pour them into a sieve to drain. Place the onions in a nonreactive container along with the apple, vinegar, the remaining ³/₄ cup water, the apple juice concentrate, juniper berries, and cinnamon stick. Allow to cool, cover, and refrigerate for at least 1 hour or for up to 4 days.

2. To prepare the salmon, place it, skin side down, in a shallow dish. In a small bowl, stir together the salt, pepper, cinnamon, and allspice. Sprinkle the mixture evenly over the flesh side of the salmon. Let the salmon rest, uncovered, in a cool place for 1 to 2 hours. Meanwhile, ready your smoker using the apple-wood twigs or chips.

3. When you are ready to begin smoking the salmon, gently brush the flesh side of the fish with the apple juice concentrate. Smoke the salmon at a fairly low temperature according to the smoker manufacturer's instructions until it is just past medium-rare (slightly translucent in the center), replenishing the smoking wood as the smoke diminishes. Remove from the smoker.

4. Meanwhile, prepare the vinaigrette: In a small bowl, whisk together all the ingredients. Taste and adjust the seasoning.

5. To serve, put the lettuce and celery in a bowl and season lightly with salt and pepper. Add the vinaigrette and toss to coat evenly. Divide the salad evenly among large dinner plates. With your fingers, pull the skin off the warm salmon and discard. Again using your fingers, break up the salmon into large flakes, discarding any errant bones, and arrange the flakes on top of the dressed lettuce. Drain the pickled onion and apple slices, discarding the brine and spices, and arrange them on top of the salmon. Serve immediately, while the salmon is still warm.

Warm White Bean Salad

SERVES 4 TO 6 *This versatile salad can be served warm or at room temperature as an accompaniment to grilled or roasted fish, chicken, pork, or lamb. It is also good with grilled vegetables for a light vegetarian meal. We use it at olive oil tastings because we feel that it shows off the flavors of our olive oil.*

1¼ cups dried navy beans or other small white beans
3 cloves garlic
1 bay leaf
Sea salt or kosher salt

vinaigrette
⅓ cup extra virgin olive oil
1 tablespoon red wine vinegar
¼ cup finely diced shallot
2 teaspoons whole-grain Dijon mustard
½ teaspoon sea salt or kosher salt
¼ teaspoon freshly ground pepper
Scant ½ teaspoon chopped fresh thyme
Scant ½ teaspoon chopped fresh marjoram
Scant ½ teaspoon chopped fresh flat-leaf parsley

½ cup finely diced red onion

1. Pick over the beans and remove any dirt or stones. Rinse the beans, place in a 3-quart saucepan, and add water to cover by 3 inches. Bring to a boil over high heat, cover, remove from the heat, and let stand for 1 hour. Drain the beans, return them to the pan, and add the garlic, bay leaf, and fresh water to cover by 2 inches. Bring to a simmer over high heat, reduce the heat to maintain a simmer, cover partially, and cook just until tender, 1 to 1½ hours. Cook the beans gently to maintain their shape, and add more water if necessary to keep the beans covered with liquid. Season to taste with salt during the last 15 minutes.

2. While the beans are cooking, prepare the vinaigrette: In a small bowl, whisk together all the ingredients. Taste and adjust the seasoning.

3. Place the onion in a large bowl. When the beans are done, drain them, discard the garlic and bay leaf, and add the beans to the bowl with the onion. Add about two-thirds of the vinaigrette and toss to mix well. (Reserve the remaining vinaigrette for marinating ahi tuna or chicken before grilling, or to dress grilled vegetables.) Taste and adjust the seasoning. Serve immediately, or let cool to room temperature before serving.

Celery Salad with Pecorino Cheese

SERVES 6 TO 8 *Crisp, moist celery and lettuce, sharp, salty pecorino cheese, and fruity, acidic lemon juice complement one another beautifully in this recipe. As always, choose the freshest, most flavorful ingredients that you can find; they are exposed in this dish and any shortcomings will be readily apparent.*

vinaigrette

½ cup extra virgin olive oil

5 tablespoons fresh lemon juice

1 shallot, finely diced

1 teaspoon grated lemon zest

½ teaspoon sea salt or kosher salt

¼ teaspoon freshly ground pepper

1 small head lettuce, preferably red leaf, leaves
    separated and torn into bite-sized pieces

Sea salt or kosher salt

Freshly ground pepper

12 celery stalks, thinly sliced

¼-pound wedge pecorino cheese

1. To prepare the vinaigrette, whisk together all the ingredients. Taste and adjust the seasoning.

2. Place the lettuce in a bowl and season lightly with salt and pepper. Drizzle about half the vinaigrette over the lettuce and toss to coat evenly. Divide the lettuce evenly among chilled salad plates. Place the celery in the same bowl and season lightly with salt and pepper. Drizzle with the remaining vinaigrette and toss to coat evenly. Using a slotted spoon, divide the celery evenly among the plates, placing each portion in a pile in the center of the lettuce. Using a vegetable peeler, shave long strips of pecorino over each salad. Spoon any vinaigrette remaining in the bowl that held the celery over the salads, then top each salad with a grind or two of pepper. Serve immediately.

Two Vinaigrettes

Lemon Vinaigrette

MAKES ABOUT 1 1/2 CUPS

1 cup extra virgin olive oil

6 tablespoons fresh lemon juice

1 to 2 teaspoons red wine vinegar

1 large shallot, finely diced

1 tablespoon grated lemon zest

1/2 teaspoon sea salt or kosher salt

1/4 teaspoon freshly ground pepper

In a small bowl, whisk together all the ingredients. Taste and adjust the seasoning.

Red Wine Vinaigrette

MAKES ABOUT 3/4 CUP

1/2 cup extra virgin olive oil

3 tablespoons red wine vinegar

1 teaspoon balsamic vinegar

2 tablespoons finely diced shallot

1/2 teaspoon sea salt or kosher salt

1/4 teaspoon freshly ground pepper

In a small bowl, whisk together all the ingredients. Taste and adjust the seasoning.

a tip on making vinaigrettes

For clarity and familiarity, I have given instructions for using a bowl and whisk when making vinaigrettes throughout this book. But I make almost all of my vinaigrettes in an 8-ounce canning jar with a metal ring band and a lid with red sealant. (The gray sealant used on some lids will not stand up to the oil.) I put in all of the ingredients, tighten the lid, and shake the jar. I then remove the lid, taste and adjust the seasoning, and replace the lid. The jar then waits on the counter until I need it. One more quick shake and it is ready for use. For me, the jar is neater, takes up less room, is easier to clean, and is just as effective as a bowl and whisk.

Fattoush

SERVES 6 *I suspect that Lebanese* fattoush *was invented to give people a way to use stale pita bread in the same way that Italians use their old bread to make* panzanella *or the English use theirs to make bread pudding. I love the crunchy pita, which contrasts with the crunch of the cucumber and onion, the juiciness of the tomato, and the acid of the lemon vinaigrette. Mix the salad shortly before serving so that it does not have a chance to soften. Add a pinch of coarsely ground, freshly toasted cumin seed with the herbs for a pleasantly aromatic accent.*

6 large pita bread rounds

3 cups ½-inch-dice vine-ripened tomato, preferably heirloom

1¼ cups ¼-inch-dice red onion

1 cup thinly sliced green onion, including light green tops

2 cups ½-inch-dice unpeeled Armenian, Japanese, or English cucumber

6 cups 1½-inch-dice romaine lettuce

¾ cup chopped fresh mint

½ cup chopped fresh flat-leaf parsley

½ cup finely shredded fresh basil

Sea salt or kosher salt

Freshly ground pepper

1¼ cups Lemon Vinaigrette (facing page)

1. Preheat the oven to 250°F. Lay the pita rounds on a baking sheet and bake, turning occasionally, until crisp, about 15 minutes. Remove from the oven, let cool, and break into chunks.

2. In a large bowl, combine the pita bread chunks, tomato, red and green onion, cucumber, lettuce, mint, parsley, and basil. Season lightly with salt and pepper. Add the Lemon Vinaigrette, toss well, and serve.

Raita

MAKES ABOUT 1 3/4 CUPS *Cooks in many countries in the eastern Mediterranean serve a version of this creamy yogurt-cucumber mixture. It makes a delicious accompaniment to grilled dishes that are assertively seasoned, its neutral, cooling flavor acting as a good counterpoint to spice and heat.*

1½ cups plain yogurt

1 cup finely diced, unpeeled Armenian, Japanese, or English cucumber

Sea salt or kosher salt

Freshly ground pepper

2 tablespoons chopped fresh mint (optional)

¾ teaspoon ground, lightly toasted cumin seeds (optional)

¼ teaspoon finely chopped garlic, or more to taste (optional)

1. Line a sieve with 4 layers of cheesecloth and put the yogurt in it. Loosely tie together the opposite corners of the cheesecloth, and pass the handle of a wooden spoon under the knots. Suspend the yogurt over a bowl in the refrigerator and allow to drain for 4 hours.

2. Pour off the liquid that has accumulated in the bowl, then combine the thickened yogurt and the cucumber in the bowl. Stir to mix well. Season to taste with salt and pepper and add the mint, cumin, and/or garlic, if desired. Serve chilled or at room temperature.

Aioli

MAKES ABOUT 1 CUP *In Provence, this garlic mayonnaise is used on many types of dishes, both hot and cold. I like to use it as a garnish for fish soups, but it is also good on sandwiches made from leftover cooked meats and for serving alongside vegetables such as asparagus and artichokes. This is a fairly tame version, so feel free to use more garlic.*

3 cloves garlic, very finely chopped

1 egg yolk

¾ cup extra virgin olive oil

1 tablespoon fresh lemon juice

½ teaspoon sea salt or kosher salt

¼ teaspoon freshly ground pepper

In a bowl, whisk together the garlic and egg yolk. Whisking constantly, add the olive oil in a thin, steady stream, very slowly at first. Once the mixture emulsifies, the oil may be added a little more quickly. Whisk in the lemon juice, salt, and pepper, then taste and adjust the seasoning. Cover and refrigerate until needed. It will keep for up to 2 days.

saving a mayonnaise

Sometimes, no matter how careful you are, a mayonnaise will break, or separate. It is possible to save it, however. Using a clean bowl and whisk, fresh oil, and another egg yolk, begin whisking oil into the yolk in a thin, steady stream. Whisk vigorously but add oil slowly at first. The addition of the first few tablespoons of oil is the critical time because a mayonnaise is particularly unstable at the very beginning, before the ingredients have emulsified. Once the emulsion has thickened enough to start holding a soft shape (after 2 or 3 tablespoons of oil have been added), begin adding the broken mayonnaise in a thin, steady stream. As the mayonnaise thickens, you can pour faster, but you must still whisk rapidly. Working in this manner, you should be able to add all of the broken mayonnaise to the new one. If it becomes too thick, add 1 or 2 teaspoons water to thin it.

Rouille

MAKES ABOUT 1¹/4 CUPS *Another Provençal version of mayonnaise, this pretty rose-tinted sauce is often used to garnish fish soups.*

2 large cloves garlic, finely chopped

1 red bell pepper, roasted and peeled (page 132), then chopped

1 thick slice French bread, crust discarded, torn into small pieces

¹/8 teaspoon red pepper flakes, or more to taste

2 to 4 teaspoons liquid from fish soup or water

1 tablespoon fresh lemon juice

1 egg yolk

¹/2 teaspoon freshly ground pepper

¹/4 teaspoon sea salt or kosher salt

³/4 cup extra virgin olive oil

In a mortar or blender, combine the garlic, bell pepper, bread, red pepper flakes, soup liquid or water, and lemon juice and pound with a pestle or process until a paste forms. Add the egg yolk, pepper, and salt and mix well. While working the pestle constantly or with the motor running, add the olive oil in a thin, steady stream, very slowly at first, as you would when making mayonnaise. Once the mixture emulsifies, the oil may be added a little more quickly. Taste and adjust the seasoning. Cover and refrigerate until needed. It will keep for up to 2 days.

Pasta, Pizza, and Focaccia

Pasta is *the* national dish of Italy and for good reason. It is incredibly satisfying in all its manifestations. I like it best at its simplest, with a sauce of olive oil with garlic, vine-ripened tomatoes, and fragrant basil (page 79) straight from the garden. If I am using dried pasta, I prefer the flavor of a good imported brand such as Rustichella d'Abruzzo. Such brands are made with hard durum wheat using traditional methods including bronze dies that give the pastas a minutely roughened surface that "holds" sauces nicely. There is also a good pasta recipe in the previous chapter that is a variation on the recipe for Mussel Soup with Swiss Chard, Tomato, and Aioli (page 40).

I sometimes think that commercially made pizza is rapidly becoming *the* national dish of the United States. However, the average pizzeria pizza is too often lost beneath a heavy load of toppings. A true Italian pizza (or the thicker focaccia) is a freshly made flat bread topped with olive oil and only a few ingredients. The simplicity of an authentic Italian pizza in which each component can be appreciated will come as a wonderful surprise for those who have never tried one. Similarly, a snack of grilled bread drizzled with olive oil or White Bean Crostini (page 95) will show off a few basic ingredients to perfection.

Spaghetti with Sun-Dried Tomatoes, Olives, and Capers

SERVES 5 AS A MAIN COURSE, OR 8 AS A FIRST COURSE *The addition of dried currants makes this classic southern Italian dish special. The combination of flavors gives the pasta an almost meaty taste. The term* pasta salad *has received a deservedly bad reputation, so I will only say that this dish is also good served cold.*

1 red onion, sliced ⅛ inch thick and julienned

3 cloves garlic, thinly sliced

¼ cup extra virgin olive oil, plus extra if needed

1 pound high-quality imported Italian spaghetti

⅔ cup oil-packed sun-dried tomatoes, drained, with oil reserved, and julienned

½ cup dry-cured black olives, pitted and julienned

2 tablespoons salt-packed capers, soaked in warm water for 10 minutes and drained

¼ cup dried currants, soaked in hot water for 10 minutes and drained

Leaves from ½ bunch fresh basil, cut into chiffonade (about 1 cup)

½ teaspoon sea salt or kosher salt

½ teaspoon coarsely ground pepper

Freshly grated Parmigiano-Reggiano cheese and/or chiffonade-cut basil for serving (optional)

1. In a small sauté pan, combine the onion, garlic, and ¼ cup olive oil over very low heat and warm for 10 minutes. The onion and garlic should not sizzle.

2. Meanwhile, cook the pasta in plenty of salted, boiling water until al dente, 8 to 12 minutes, or according to package directions. While the pasta is cooking, finish preparing the sauce.

3. In a large, warmed bowl, combine the onion mixture, tomatoes, olives, capers, currants, basil, salt, and pepper. Measure the oil reserved from the tomatoes and add extra virgin olive oil as needed to total ¼ cup. Add to the bowl and mix together well.

4. When the pasta is ready, drain it, add to the sauce, and toss to coat well. Divide among warmed individual bowls. Top with the cheese and/or basil, if desired, and serve at once.

Rigatoni with Artichokes and Pancetta

SERVES 5 AS A MAIN COURSE, OR 8 AS A FIRST COURSE *The combination of artichokes and pancetta is a great one. Here, onion, garlic, and olives round out the flavor. The optional tomatoes make this into a saucy American-style dish. Made without them, the dish is drier, and thus more Italian in style. Most baby artichokes are too small to have formed a fuzzy choke. If you find some with a choke, or if you want to use larger artichokes, use a sharp-tipped paring knife or small spoon to remove the prickly centers.*

3 cups water

Juice of 1 small lemon

1½ pounds (12 to 18) baby artichokes

4 tablespoons extra virgin olive oil

½ teaspoon sea salt or kosher salt

½ teaspoon coarsely ground pepper

¼ pound pancetta, sliced ¼ inch thick and the slices unrolled and cut crosswise into ½-inch-wide strips

1 large red onion, about ½ pound, cut in half lengthwise and sliced crosswise ¼ inch thick

3 cloves garlic, thinly sliced

⅔ cup dry-cured black olives, pitted and roughly chopped

1 can (14 ounces) plum tomatoes, roughly chopped, with juice (optional)

1 pound high-quality imported Italian rigatoni

¾ cup freshly grated Parmigiano-Reggiano cheese

1. Fill a bowl with the water and add the lemon juice. Trim off one-third of the top of each artichoke, then trim off the darkened stem end. Snap off the outer leaves until you reach the tender, yellow-green inner leaves. Trim off any remaining dark green parts. Cut each artichoke in half lengthwise. To retard browning, drop the halves into the bowl of lemon water.

2. In a large, heavy sauté pan, heat 1 tablespoon of the olive oil over medium-high heat. Add the artichokes with enough of the lemon water to half cover them and add ¼ teaspoon each of the salt and the pepper (discard the remaining lemon water). Reduce the heat to medium-low, cover partially, and braise until the artichokes are just tender, about 7 minutes. Drain the artichokes, reserving ½ cup of the braising liquid. Reserve the artichokes and liquid separately.

continued

3. Return the pan to medium-low heat and add 1 tablespoon of the olive oil and the pancetta. Cook, stirring occasionally, until the pancetta is golden brown, about 5 minutes. Add 1 tablespoon more of the olive oil and the onion, increase the heat to medium-high, and continue cooking, stirring often, until the onion starts to color, about 5 minutes. Reduce the heat to low and add the garlic, olives, braised artichokes, tomatoes (if using), and the remaining ¼ teaspoon each salt and pepper. Continue to cook over low heat, stirring occasionally, while you cook the pasta.

4. Cook the pasta in plenty of salted, boiling water until al dente, 10 to 12 minutes, or according to package directions. Drain the pasta and add it to the sauce along with the remaining 1 tablespoon olive oil and the reserved ½ cup braising liquid. Stir to combine.

5. Divide the pasta among warmed bowls. Top with the cheese, dividing it evenly, and serve at once.

VARIATION: *Bacon can be used in place of the pancetta. Use thick-sliced, naturally smoked bacon and cut the slices crosswise into ½-inch-wide strips. Omit the 1 tablespoon of olive oil for cooking, as the bacon will render enough of its own fat, and pour off the accumulated fat once the bacon is golden brown.*

Spaghetti with Fresh Tomatoes, Basil, Garlic, and Olive Oil

SERVES 5 AS A MAIN COURSE, OR 8 AS A FIRST COURSE *I use a mixture of red, orange, and yellow heirloom tomatoes for this dish, adding zebra-striped green tomatoes if they happen to be available. It all depends on what Margaret has in the kitchen garden. Don't be put off by the amount of garlic, as the slow warming in olive oil mellows the flavor.*

2 small heads garlic, separated into cloves, peeled, and thinly sliced

½ cup extra virgin olive oil

1 pound high-quality imported Italian spaghetti

1½ pounds assorted vine-ripened heirloom tomatoes (see recipe introduction), cut into ⅜-inch dice

½ pound assorted vine-ripened cherry tomatoes, cut in half

Leaves from ½ bunch fresh basil, cut in chiffonade (about 1 cup)

½ teaspoon sea salt or kosher salt

½ teaspoon coarsely ground pepper

Freshly grated Parmigiano-Reggiano cheese and/or additional chiffonade-cut basil for serving (optional)

1. In a small sauté pan, combine the garlic and ¼ cup of the olive oil over very low heat and warm for 10 minutes. The garlic should not sizzle.

2. Meanwhile, cook the pasta in plenty of salted, boiling water until al dente, 8 to 12 minutes, or according to package directions. While the pasta is cooking, finish preparing the sauce.

3. In a large, warmed bowl, combine the garlic mixture, tomatoes, basil, salt, pepper, and the remaining ¼ cup oil and mix well.

4. When the pasta is ready, drain it, add it to the sauce, and toss to coat well. Divide among warmed individual bowls. Garnish with the cheese and/or basil, if desired.

Fresh Pasta

MAKES ABOUT ½ POUND, SERVES 2 TO 4 *This is a basic pasta recipe that can be finished in many ways. It results in a dough that is drier than most, which makes it a little harder to form into a cohesive unit for rolling. But this drier character also makes the dough easier to handle once it is cut into shape. It is best made on a roller-type pasta machine. Most pasta machines have cutters of two different widths in addition to the rollers. You can use the pasta uncut as lasagna, or use one of the cutters to form fettuccine or tagliarini. If you would like your pasta cut to a different width, cut the sheets to the length that you would like, dust them lightly with rice flour (use regular Asian rice flour, not sweet or glutinous rice flour), roll up each sheet loosely, and then cut crosswise with a sharp knife to whatever width you like. Think of your sauce when deciding how thick to roll and how wide to cut your pasta. In general, the lighter the texture of the sauce, the thinner and/or narrower the pasta.*

Fresh pasta should be cooked within a few hours of when it is made. If stored in its original, moist state, it will begin to pick up off flavors from the environment, which will be evident when cooked. However, you can dry fresh pasta right after it is made (as egg noodles are) with good results. Drape the strands of pasta over dowels or kitchen-cabinet doors protected with clean towels. Dry the strands until they are completely brittle, about 4 hours, depending on the humidity. They will keep well, tightly covered, for several months.

1 cup unbleached all-purpose flour

¼ cup fine semolina flour (or additional all-purpose flour)

½ teaspoon sea salt or kosher salt

2 large eggs

White rice flour for dusting cut pasta

4 quarts water and 1 tablespoon sea salt or kosher salt for cooking

1. Combine the all-purpose flour, semolina flour, and salt in a food processor and pulse twice to mix. Add the eggs, pulse several more times until combined, and then process until the dough begins to come together, 10 to 15 seconds. Pulse several more times until the dough separates into granules. Ideally at this point the dough will be in granules the size of couscous. If the dough is too wet and has not separated, add more all-purpose flour 1 tablespoon at a time, pulsing between additions, until the dough has the desired appearance. Test the dough by squeezing a small handful. It should hold together when released without being too sticky. If the dough is too dry, add water 1 teaspoon at a time, pulsing after each addition until it barely holds together.

2. Divide the dough granules evenly between 2 sheets of plastic wrap. Press each portion firmly with the heel of your hand to help the granules adhere to one another, forming each portion into a 4-by-6-inch rectangle. Wrap each rectangle tightly in the plastic wrap. Let rest at room temperature for 30 minutes to 1 hour.

3. Work with 1 dough rectangle at a time. Set the rollers on your pasta machine at the widest setting and pass the dough through the rollers. After each pass through the machine, fold the dough in half horizontally and run it through again. This dough is on the dry side and may need folding a few times to form a cohesive sheet. Once the dough has come together, fold the ends of the sheet in to meet in the middle, rotate the dough 90 degrees, and send it through the rollers. After 6 passes in this fashion, stop folding the dough, tighten the setting of the rollers by one number, and run the dough through the rollers again. Tighten the rollers again and repeat until the dough is as thin as you like. Then pass the dough through the cutters, choosing whichever width you want. Toss the cut pasta in a little rice flour to keep it from sticking together. Repeat with the remaining rectangle.

4. To cook the pasta, bring the water and salt to a rapid boil in a large pot. Gently add the pasta and stir to keep the strands from sticking together. It is difficult to give a cooking time due to the variables of thickness and width, but a very thin, soft cut could take as little as $1^{1}/_{2}$ minutes, while a thick, drier cut could take 8 to 10 minutes.

Gnocchi

SERVES 6 *There are many different opinions on how to make the best gnocchi. Mark has found, through research and trial and error, that this is the easiest and best way to do it. Use older potatoes, bake them instead of boiling them, use a food mill, and handle the dough as little as possible. These factors all help to keep the moisture level low and ensure that your gnocchi are as light as possible. Using the back of a cheese grater to form the gnocchi was Maurizio's contribution. Most recipes suggest using a fork for shaping them, which produces four or five grooves on the outside surface. When you use a cheese grater, however, the gnocchi have a more intricate pattern of raised bumps, which greatly increases their sauce-holding propensities. We have tried many different graters and have found that the kind with medium perforations designed for grating hard Parmesan cheese works the best.*

Serve the gnocchi with Tomato Sauce (page 84), Italian Sausage and Tomato Sauce (page 85), or with melted butter, freshly grated Parmigiano-Reggiano cheese, and a few leaves of fresh sage or basil.

1 pound large red potatoes

1 medium egg

1 tablespoon sea salt or kosher salt

1 teaspoon freshly ground white pepper

1¼ cups unbleached all-purpose flour, or a little more

4 quarts water and 1 tablespoon sea salt or kosher salt for cooking

1. Preheat the oven to 375°F. Poke the potatoes a few times with a fork to prevent the skins from bursting, and place them directly on the oven rack. Bake the potatoes until they are soft when you squeeze them with your fingers, about 50 minutes. (Protect your hand with an oven mitt.) Remove from the oven and let cool.

2. Peel the potatoes and pass them through a potato ricer or the medium screen of a food mill placed over a large bowl. Make a well in the middle of the potatoes. In a small bowl, lightly beat the egg with the salt and pepper, and pour into the well. Using a fork, gradually mix the potato into the egg mixture by pulling the potato into the well. Using a wooden spoon, mix 1¼ cups flour into the potato mixture. Do not overmix. If the mixture is sticky, add only enough extra flour as needed to eliminate the stickiness.

3. Transfer the dough to a lightly floured work surface and knead it for a couple of turns. Work the dough as little as possible. Cut the dough into pieces the size of a small orange and roll each piece into a long strand about ½ inch in diameter. Cut each strand into ¾-inch-long pieces. Press each piece onto the sharp side of a flat cheese grater, gently pushing down with your thumb as you remove it, thus flattening the dough and forming a slight hollow on the inner surface. Set the gnocchi aside on a lightly floured tray.

4. To cook the gnocchi, bring the water and salt to a rapid boil in a large pot. Gently add the gnocchi, stirring at the beginning to keep them from sticking. The gnocchi will rise to the surface after a few seconds. Cook for another minute and then skim the cooked gnocchi from the pot with a wire skimmer or a slotted spoon. Serve the gnocchi as suggested in the recipe introduction.

Tomato Sauce

MAKES ABOUT 6 CUPS *Margaret provides us with so many tomatoes that we find ourselves cooking hundreds of pounds of various varieties into purées that we then freeze. The garden also gives us a bounty of plum tomatoes that we dry or, best of all, put up in quart and pint jars to use year-round. One of our favorite things to cook at the ranch is pizza in the wood-burning oven. This tomato sauce of Mark's makes an excellent pizza sauce if you cook it until it becomes thick. It is also great on Gnocchi (page 82), Fresh Pasta (page 80), roasted eggplant with melted mozzarella, or just about anything else that calls for tomato sauce. The anchovy adds depth and character to the sauce, but not an obvious flavor, so do not be hesitant about adding it.*

½ cup extra virgin olive oil

1 yellow onion, finely diced

3 cloves garlic, chopped

½ cup dry red wine

1 salt-packed anchovy, filleted and rinsed

1 can (28 ounces) tomato purée

1 can (28 ounces) plum tomatoes, drained and liquid reserved

1½ teaspoons sea salt or kosher salt

½ teaspoon red pepper flakes

Julienned fresh basil or chopped fresh oregano leaves

1. Preheat a heavy, 4-quart saucepan over medium heat. Add ¼ cup of the olive oil and the onion and cook, stirring frequently with a wooden spoon, until the onion is just translucent, about 10 minutes. If the onion starts to brown, reduce the heat. Add the garlic and stir for 10 seconds or so, being careful not to let it brown. Increase the heat to medium, add the red wine, and cook until almost evaporated. Add the anchovy fillets and break it up with the wooden spoon. Add the tomato purée and plum tomatoes, increase the heat to medium-high, and bring the mixture to a boil, stirring frequently and breaking up the tomatoes. Reduce the heat to low and cook gently for 20 to 30 minutes to blend the flavors.

2. Add the salt, red pepper flakes, and the remaining ¼ cup olive oil and stir to combine. Taste and adjust the seasoning. If the sauce has become too thick, add the reserved tomato liquid. Use immediately, or let cool, cover tightly, and store in the refrigerator for up to 5 days or in the freezer for up to 6 months. Add the fresh herbs to taste just before serving—I like to use basil with pizza or gnocchi and oregano with pasta.

Italian Sausage and Tomato Sauce

MAKES ABOUT 8 CUPS *This sauce is another of Mark's excellent recipes. The sausage, onion, and tomato provide textural contrast, spice, and acidity, and are a perfect foil to gnocchi or rigatoni. Sweet Italian sausages are commonly flavored with fennel seeds, dried oregano, and wine, and are available made with pork, lamb, chicken, or turkey. We always use pork, with lamb the second choice.*

½ cup extra virgin olive oil

2 pounds sweet Italian sausage, cut into 1-inch pieces with casings intact

1 yellow onion, sliced ⅛ inch thick

3 cloves garlic, minced

½ cup dry red wine

1 can (28 ounces) plum tomatoes, drained and liquid reserved

1 can (28 ounces) tomato purée

Leaves from 12 fresh thyme sprigs, chopped

Leaves from 6 fresh oregano sprigs, chopped

1 teaspoon sea salt or kosher salt

¼ teaspoon red pepper flakes

2 red bell peppers, roasted and peeled (page 132), then cut lengthwise into strips ¼ inch wide

1. Preheat a large skillet over medium-high heat. Add ¼ cup of the olive oil and the sausage pieces and cook, turning as needed with a wooden spoon, until browned on all sides, about 5 minutes. Using a slotted spoon, transfer the sausage pieces to a bowl. Reduce the heat to medium-low and add the remaining ¼ cup olive oil and the onion. Cook, stirring frequently with the wooden spoon, until the onion is just translucent, about 10 minutes. If the onion starts to brown, reduce the heat. Add the garlic and stir for 10 seconds or so, being careful not to let it brown. Add the wine, plum tomatoes, and tomato purée, increase the heat to medium, and bring to a boil, stirring frequently and breaking up the tomatoes. Reduce the heat to a slow simmer and cook for about 10 minutes to blend the flavors.

2. Return the sausage pieces to the pan, add the thyme, oregano, salt, red pepper flakes, and pepper strips, and stir to combine. Taste and adjust the seasoning. If the sauce has become too thick, add the reserved tomato liquid. Use immediately, or let cool, cover tightly, and store in the refrigerator for up to 5 days or in the freezer for up to 6 months.

Pizza Dough

MAKES TWO 12-INCH ROUNDS *For the best crust, it is important to keep the dough as moist as possible by adding the minimum amount of extra flour during mixing. As a general rule, the wetter the dough, the moister and more tender the result. The small quantity of rye flour gives the crust a more interesting flavor without affecting its texture. Shaping pizza dough into a perfect circle is a skill that improves with practice. Do not be discouraged if your first attempts are shaped like Idaho or Texas; they will still taste great. Any small tears in the dough circles can be repaired by folding the damaged part over a nearby intact area. Have your oven preheated and all your toppings at hand before shaping the dough. Wood-fired ovens make the best-textured pizzas, but a baking stone preheated in a regular oven is a good alternative. If you don't have either, preheat an inverted, heavy-duty baking sheet instead.*

A recipe for pizza topped with heirloom tomatoes, mozzarella and Parmigiano-Reggiano cheeses, and basil follows, but many other possibilities exist. For example, spread a thin layer of Tomato Sauce (page 84) on the dough and top with a small amount of shredded mozzarella cheese and a few anchovies, some capers, and a sprinkling of red pepper flakes and dried oregano, or with some thinly sliced mushrooms. Thinly sliced cured meats such as salami or pepperoni can also be added, as can crumbled, cooked sausage. Other vegetables, such as raw asparagus, braised artichokes, roasted bell peppers (page 132), or onions, are also good on pizza. I think it is better to put a few well-chosen ingredients on each pizza, rather than loading them with too many disparate items.

sponge

½ cup lukewarm water

2 teaspoons active dry yeast

½ cup rye flour or whole-wheat flour

dough

¾ cup plus 2 tablespoons lukewarm water

1 tablespoon extra virgin olive oil, plus extra for the bowl and for forming

1 teaspoon sea salt or kosher salt

3¼ cups unbleached all-purpose flour, plus extra if needed

Yellow cornmeal for dusting baker's peel

1. To prepare the sponge, place the water in a large, deep bowl. Sprinkle the yeast over the water and then stir in the rye or whole-wheat flour. Cover and leave in a warm place until very bubbly, 20 to 30 minutes.

2. To prepare the dough, add the water, 1 tablespoon olive oil, the salt, and 3 1/4 cups all-purpose flour to the sponge mixture. Mix with a wooden spoon, adding more flour if necessary to make a moist dough. Turn out onto a lightly floured work surface and knead until smooth and elastic, about 10 minutes. Add more water or flour as necessary to maintain a moist, slightly sticky dough. Put the dough into a bowl that has been rubbed with olive oil, and turn the dough to coat it completely with the oil. Cover the bowl with plastic wrap and leave in a warm place until the dough has doubled in size, about 1 hour.

3. Punch down the dough and let rest for 20 minutes. Transfer the dough to a lightly floured work surface and divide the dough in half. Using your palms and cupped fingers, roll each half into a smooth ball. Place both balls on a lightly oiled surface and turn the balls to coat completely. Cover with plastic wrap and let rest for 15 minutes before using, or refrigerate for up to 4 hours.

4. If you would like to make the dough a day in advance, reroll the balls after they have rested for 15 minutes, lightly oil them, and refrigerate, tightly covered, until ready to use. Take them out of the refrigerator 30 minutes before you want to form the pizzas.

5. To form a pizza crust, have ready a cornmeal-dusted baker's peel or inverted baking sheet, a small bowl holding a little flour, and a lightly floured work surface. Lightly flour your hands, pick up 1 ball, and dip it into the bowl of flour. Using the thumb and fingertips of both hands, starting in the center of the ball and holding it just above the work surface, lightly pinch and squeeze the dough while turning it constantly. Gradually flatten it, while working toward the rim, into a disk 10 to 12 inches in diameter. If your hands or the dough become sticky, lay the dough on the floured surface, flour your hands again, and resume shaping. Lay the shaped dough on the prepared baker's peel or baking sheet, top as desired, and bake as directed in the following recipe.

Heirloom Tomato Pizza

SERVES 1 *Pizza doesn't get any more simple—or any more delicious—than this. Its success hinges on the quality of the ingredients.*

1 Pizza Dough ball, shaped as directed and placed on a baker's peel (page 86)

1 tablespoon extra virgin olive oil

Sea salt or kosher salt

Freshly ground pepper

½ cup (2 ounces) shredded fresh mozzarella cheese

1 large heirloom tomato, cut into about 10 slices each ⅛ inch thick

3 to 4 tablespoons freshly grated Parmigiano-Reggiano cheese

1 tablespoon torn fresh basil leaves

1. Place a baking stone or inverted baking sheet in the top third of your oven and preheat the oven to 475°F. Brush the dough round lightly with the olive oil and sprinkle with about ¼ teaspoon each salt and pepper. Spread the mozzarella evenly over the round, and top with the tomato slices in a single layer. Sprinkle with 2 tablespoons Parmigiano-Reggiano cheese and a little more salt and pepper.

2. Slide the dough off the peel onto the hot baking stone or inverted baking sheet. Bake until the crust is golden at the edges and the cheese has melted, 5 to 10 minutes. Remove from the oven and top with the basil and 1 or 2 more tablespoons Parmigiano-Reggiano cheese. Serve immediately.

Focaccia Dough

MAKES ONE 11-BY-17-INCH SHEET *This dough is similar to the Pizza Dough (page 86), and the comments that appear with the latter apply here as well. I usually add some of our bread starter to this recipe. I find that it gives the crust a fuller flavor and contributes to greater oven spring when baked. If you have some starter and would like to try adding some, add 1 cup fairly dry starter to the sponge and decrease the amount of bread flour and water to 2 cups each.*

sponge

2 ¾ cups lukewarm water

2 teaspoons active dry yeast

½ cup rye flour or whole-wheat flour

3 cups unbleached bread flour

dough

1 tablespoon sea salt or kosher salt

½ cup hot water, plus extra if needed

⅓ cup extra virgin olive oil, plus extra for bowl and pan

3 cups unbleached all-purpose flour, plus extra if needed

1. To prepare the sponge, place the water, yeast, rye or whole-wheat flour, and bread flour in the bowl of a stand mixer and stir to mix well. Cover and leave in a warm place for 1 hour.

2. To prepare the dough, in a small bowl, combine the salt and hot water and let cool. Stir in the ⅓ cup olive oil, and then add the oil mixture and the all-purpose flour to the sponge. Fit the stand mixer with the paddle attachment, and mix on low speed, adding more flour as necessary, until the mixture forms a ball and begins to clear the sides and bottom of the bowl. Change to the bread hook attachment and knead on low speed for 5 minutes, adding more water or all-purpose flour as necessary to maintain a moist, slightly sticky dough. Add 1 tablespoon olive oil to the bowl and turn the dough in the bowl so that it is coated with oil on all sides. Cover the bowl with plastic wrap and leave in a warm place until the dough has doubled in size, 2 to 3 hours.

3. Punch the dough down in the bowl and let rest for 15 minutes. Coat the bottom and sides of a rimmed 11-by-17-inch baking sheet with olive oil. Place down the dough in the pan and, using your fingertips, pull and stretch the dough to cover the bottom of the pan evenly. Cover with plastic wrap and let rest for 15 minutes. If after that time the dough has shrunk away from the sides of the pan, gently stretch it back into place. Using your fingertips, deeply dimple the surface of the dough.

4. Top the focaccia as desired, and bake as directed in the following recipe.

Making Bread without Kneading

For some time, I have been experimenting with mixing yeast doughs without the aid of a mixer and without traditional kneading. In an effort to keep my doughs moist and thus more tender when baked, I added extra water, but I soon found that the stand mixer's dough hook was no longer able to form the dough into a kneadable mass that cleaned the sides of the bowl. In talking with other bakers, most notably the Webbers of nearby Petaluma's excellent Della Fattoria, I discovered that it is possible to mix doughs by hand and even to forgo kneading some of them.

My process is simple. I use it for the loaves of bread that we bake each day at the ranch and for pizza and focaccia doughs. This description is a good basis for experimentation, and I urge you to give it a try if you are already comfortable with preparing a standard yeast dough. I use the handled bowl from a stand mixer and a sturdy metal spoon from start to finish. Early in the process, when gluten strands have yet to form, you are stirring what looks like a batter. As the gluten strands develop and lengthen, raise the spoon higher above the surface of the batter, stretching the gluten. As the repeated stretching continues, the dough will become smoother and more cohesive and finally (after 6 to 10 minutes) form a rather loose mass that resists sticking to the bowl. At this point I allow the dough to rise until double and then turn the mass out onto a floured surface and allow it to rest for 10 minutes. I then halve the dough and begin forming it by folding and stretching each piece in on itself like a business letter. I do this three or four times, rotating the dough 90 degrees each time. I leave both portions, smooth side up, on the floured surface for about 20 minutes, then finish forming the loaves and leave them to rise. The gentle stretching combined with the gradual shaping results in a chewy, flavorful loaf with larger vacuoles and a thinner, more tender crust. The same benefits occur in pizza and focaccia dough.

Focaccia with Peaches, Red Onions, and Sage

MAKES ONE 11-BY-17-INCH FOCACCIA *The Italian word* focaccia *comes from the Latin* focus, *or "hearth," which the ancient Romans considered to be the center of the home. The topping can be as simple as a sprinkling of coarse salt with herbs or a scattering of caramelized onion with Parmigiano-Reggiano cheese, or as tantalizing as this combination of peaches and red onion. Cut into small squares, focaccia makes a good appetizer or, with the addition of a salad and a slice or two of prosciutto, a tasty light meal.*

Focaccia Dough (page 90)

topping

3 firm but ripe peaches

1 tablespoon plus ¼ cup extra virgin olive oil

2 red onions, sliced ⅛ inch thick

2 tablespoons red wine vinegar

1 teaspoon sea salt or kosher salt

4 tablespoons firmly packed light brown sugar

1½ teaspoons finely julienned fresh sage

1. Prepare the dough and leave to rise until doubled in size.

2. To prepare the topping, bring a saucepan filled with water to a boil. Add the peaches and blanch just until the skins loosen, about 30 seconds. Drain the peaches, plunge them into ice water until cool, and then peel. Halve the peaches, discard the pits, and slice ¼ inch thick.

3. Preheat a 10-inch sauté pan over high heat. Add the 1 tablespoon olive oil and the onions and cook, tossing frequently, until the onions are slightly softened and beginning to caramelize, about 3 minutes. Add 1 tablespoon of the vinegar and ½ teaspoon of the salt and stir for 30 seconds. Remove the onions from the pan and let cool.

4. Punch down the dough, then line the pan and dimple as directed.

5. To top the focaccia, in a small bowl, combine the peaches, the remaining 1 tablespoon vinegar, and 2 tablespoons of the sugar and stir to mix. Sprinkle the sage evenly over the dimpled dough. Drain the peaches, reserving 2 tablespoons of the liquid, and arrange the peach slices evenly over the surface of the dough. Arrange the reserved onions evenly over the peaches. Drizzle the remaining ¼ cup olive oil and the reserved peach liquid evenly over the top, and then sprinkle evenly with the remaining 2 tablespoons sugar and ½ teaspoon salt. Let the dough rise for 20 to 30 minutes. Meanwhile, preheat the oven to 425°F.

6. Bake the focaccia until it is cooked through and golden brown at the edges, 30 to 40 minutes. Remove from the oven, let cool slightly, cut into portions, and serve hot, or let cool to room temperature before cutting.

Bruschetta and Fettunta

In Italy, the first use of the *olio nuovo* from each harvest is on bruschetta. This rustic treat, which is known as *fettunta* in Tuscany and Umbria, consists of crusty country bread that is sliced and toasted over hot coals, rubbed with a clove of garlic, and drizzled liberally with the new oil. It is often prepared at the *frantoio* (olive mill) so that the olive growers can taste their minutes-old oil at its freshest.

In this country, bruschetta and its close cousins, crostini, have come to mean almost any appetizer or snack served on toasted bread, such as the White Bean Crostini on the facing page. Some other good choices for toppings include sliced mushrooms sautéed with herbs and olive oil, diced heirloom tomatoes with basil and a pinch of salt, thin slabs of fresh mozzarella cheese, or *tapenade* (olive paste). One thing these toppings have in common is that they are all greatly improved by a generous splash of flavorful olive oil.

White Bean Crostini

MAKES 32; SERVES 8 *Here, white beans are blended with lusty, peppery Tuscan—or Tuscan-style—extra virgin olive oil to wonderful advantage. Grilling the bread will produce a superior flavor, although toasting it in the oven is fine if you do not want to fire up the grill. Serve the crostini at room temperature for the best flavor.*

bean purée

1 cup dried navy beans or other small white beans
1 large clove garlic
1 fresh rosemary sprig, 3 inches long
1 fresh winter savory sprig, 2 inches long (optional)
½ teaspoon sea salt or kosher salt
¼ teaspoon freshly ground pepper
2 tablespoons extra virgin olive oil

8 slices day-old country-style bread, each about
   7 inches long by 4 inches wide by ½ inch thick,
   grilled or toasted and each slice cut into 4 triangles
Sea salt or kosher salt for serving
Extra virgin olive oil for serving

1. To prepare the bean purée, pick over the beans and remove any dirt or stones. Rinse the beans, place in a 2-quart saucepan, and add water to cover by 3 inches. Bring to a boil over high heat, cover, remove from the heat, and let stand for 1 hour. Drain the beans, return them to the pan, and add enough fresh water to cover by 2 inches. Bring to a simmer over high heat and add the garlic, rosemary, and winter savory (if using). Reduce the heat to low, cover partially, and simmer gently until tender, 1 to 1½ hours. Stir occasionally and add more water as necessary to keep the beans submerged. Add the salt and pepper, remove from the heat, and let cool to room temperature.

2. Drain the beans, reserving the liquid and discarding the stems from the herb sprig(s). Transfer the beans to a bowl, add the olive oil, and mash with a spoon or potato masher to make a rough purée. Add as much of the reserved cooking liquid as necessary to produce a purée that will just hold its shape when mounded. Taste and adjust the seasoning. The mixture should remain slightly under salted to compensate for the salt that is added once the crostini are assembled.

3. To assemble the crostini, top each bread triangle with an equal amount of the bean purée. Sprinkle with salt, drizzle with oil, and serve at room temperature.

Fish and Shellfish

McEvoy Ranch is barely eleven miles from the Pacific Ocean, and we feel its marine influence in the seasonal fogs that roll in over the hills to our west, bringing a faint salty tang to the air. I serve quite a bit of seafood, partially because it feels right this close to the ocean, and partially because it is lighter and more easily digested. Much of the day-to-day cooking I do is for lunch, and we need to be able to return to work refreshed and not overstuffed. We never tire of salmon, and when it's available, I buy wild king salmon line-caught off the coast. It has a finer flavor and texture than farmed salmon, and it goes on the grill for Pan-Seared Salmon with Olive Oil Emulsion Sauce (page 107), among other dishes. Fat mussels are another favorite, and I like to serve them when licorice-scented fennel appears in the garden, in the form of Mussels with Fennel, Blood Orange, and Pernod (page 103).

I find that homemade fish stock or fumet (page 108) makes an enormous difference when preparing fish and seafood. Try it once, and you'll see what I mean. True, it is a little extra trouble, but the results are worth it, and you can freeze small containers of it for later use.

Salt Cod with Potatoes, Leeks, and Saffron

SERVES 6 TO 8 *A staple of Mediterranean Lenten menus, salt cod can be found in Italian and Spanish food stores. Although whole sides of cod with a few pieces of skin and some bits of bone still attached are dry as a board and do not look very promising, I have found that they have the best flavor when rehydrated and cooked. However, the neatly filleted and moister salt cod found in small wooden boxes in many supermarkets is much easier to use and has a fine flavor. You will need to start soaking the fish 1 to 2 days before you plan to serve it.*

1¼ pounds skinless salt cod fillet

3 cups ½-inch-dice leek, white and light green
   parts only

¼ cup extra virgin olive oil

¼ teaspoon sea salt or kosher salt

1½ cups dry white wine

Scant ½ teaspoon lightly packed saffron threads

½ teaspoon freshly ground pepper

3 quarts Fish Fumet (page 108) or reconstituted
   frozen fish stock

¾ pound small red potatoes, unpeeled, cut into
   ½-inch dice

1 can (28 ounces) plum tomatoes, drained and diced

Freshly ground pepper for serving

¾ cup Rouille (page 70)

1. Place the cod in a large bowl, add water to cover, and refrigerate for 24 to 36 hours, changing the water 4 or 5 times. The fish should be salty to the taste but not unpleasantly so, and fairly tender in the thickest part of the fillet. Drain the cod and trim off any errant bits of skin, bones, or connective tissue. Cut the fish into bite-sized chunks and reserve until needed.

2. In a sauté pan, combine the leek, olive oil, and salt over low heat. Cover and sweat, stirring occasionally, until softened but not colored, 10 to 15 minutes. Remove from the heat and set aside.

3. In a small saucepan, bring the wine to a boil over high heat and boil until reduced by half, about 4 minutes. Remove from the heat. Crumble the saffron between your fingers into the wine, then add the pepper. Reserve until needed.

4. In a heavy, 4-quart pot, bring the fumet or stock to a simmer over high heat. Add the potatoes, reduce the heat to maintain a simmer, and cook until nearly done, about 15 minutes. Add the reserved cod, leeks, wine-saffron mixture, and the tomatoes and continue to simmer until the cod is tender, about 5 minutes.

5. Taste and adjust the seasoning immediately before serving, as salt will continue to come out of the cod while it cooks. Ladle into warmed bowls and top each serving with a few grinds of pepper and a generous spoonful of Rouille. Serve immediately.

VARIATION: *Add 4 cups chopped kale with the cod.*

Roast Salmon with Mustard

SERVES 6 *A popular dish that was served at Jan Birnbaum's Catahoula Restaurant in Calistoga, California, inspired this recipe. At the ranch, as at Catahoula, this dish is cooked in the wood-fired oven, where the glaze browns to a rich mahogany color. At home, a hot oven substitutes satisfactorily, but the glaze does not brown as much. When reduced, the apple juice concentrate develops an intense combination of tart and sweet that, when mixed with mustard and pepper, packs a lot of flavor into a thin layer. The remaining glaze is combined with the liquid from the fish and olive oil to make a light sauce that echoes the glaze.*

½ cup frozen apple juice concentrate

3 tablespoons whole-grain Dijon mustard

1 tablespoon coarsely ground pepper

4 cups Fish Fumet (page 108) or reconstituted
   frozen fish stock

1½ cups dry white wine

1 celery stalk, sliced

2 large shallots, sliced

1 teaspoon peppercorns

6 skinless pieces salmon fillet, 5 to 6 ounces each

Sea salt or kosher salt

20 to 30 baby carrots, peeled

½ cup *haricots verts,* trimmed

½ cup extra virgin olive oil

⅓ cup brine-cured French or Italian green olives,
   pitted and sliced

1. In a small saucepan, bring the apple juice concentrate to a boil over medium heat and boil until reduced by one-third, about 5 minutes. Add the mustard and ground pepper and stir to form a thick, sticky paste. Remove from the heat and reserve until needed.

2. Preheat the oven to 475°F. Oil a shallow baking pan large enough to hold the fillets in one layer.

3. In a saucepan, combine the fumet or stock, wine, celery, shallots, and peppercorns over high heat, bring to a boil, and boil until reduced to 2 cups, about 12 minutes. Strain through a fine-mesh sieve and keep warm.

4. Using one-half of the mustard paste, coat the tops of the salmon fillets. Arrange the fillets in the prepared pan. Carefully pour one-half of the wine reduction around the salmon and then salt the fish lightly. Roast the salmon until medium-rare when tested with a fork, about 7 minutes. Remove the salmon from the oven and place the fillets on warmed dinner plates.

continued

5. While the salmon is roasting, bring a large saucepan filled with salted water (1 tablespoon of salt per quart of water) to a boil over high heat, add the carrots, and boil just until tender, about 4 minutes. Using a slotted spoon, remove the carrots from the pan, and keep warm. Cook the *haricots verts* in the same boiling water until tender, about 1 minute, then drain and keep warm.

6. Pour the liquid in the baking pan into a blender and add the remaining wine reduction and mustard paste. With the motor running at medium speed, slowly pour in the olive oil in a thin, steady stream through the small hole in the center of the lid. Taste and adjust the seasoning. Surround each fillet with the olives, beans, and carrots. Pour the sauce on top of the vegetables. Serve at once.

Mussels with Fennel, Blood Orange, and Pernod

SERVES 4 *This recipe, like many in this book, was inspired by the wonderful produce that Margaret and her crew provide for us on a daily basis. On the day that this recipe was created, we had both beautiful tart-sweet blood oranges and some perfectly juicy, crunchy fennel on hand, and I decided to use them in combination with plump mussels and a splash of Pernod to echo the aroma of the fennel. If blood oranges are unavailable, substitute fresh orange juice from Valencia or another of the juicing oranges. Their juice will always have a better flavor than the juice of navel oranges. Conversely, the zest of navels will always have a truer "orange" flavor than that of juicing oranges. Tangerines and tangelos are also good substitutes for blood oranges in this recipe.*

3 tablespoons extra virgin olive oil

1 red onion, thinly sliced

1 large shallot, thinly sliced

2 cloves garlic, thinly sliced

1 large fennel bulb, trimmed, cored, and thinly sliced

1½ teaspoons fennel seeds, toasted in a dry pan
  and ground

¼ teaspoon red pepper flakes

¼ teaspoon sea salt or kosher salt

1 cup fresh blood orange juice

1 cup dry white wine

2 pounds mussels, scrubbed and debearded

2 tablespoons Pernod

1 teaspoon grated blood or navel orange zest

Freshly ground pepper for serving

4 slices country-style bread, each about 7 inches long
  by 4 inches wide by ¾ inch thick, grilled or toasted
  and each slice cut into 4 triangles

1. In a large, shallow pan, combine 1 tablespoon of the olive oil, the onion, shallot, garlic, and fennel over medium heat. Cook for a few minutes until the fennel begins to soften. Add the fennel seeds, red pepper flakes, salt, orange juice, and wine, increase the heat to high, and cook until reduced by half, about 4 minutes. Add the mussels, cover, and continue to cook over high heat, shaking the pan occasionally, until most of the mussels have opened, 3 to 4 minutes.

2. Remove the pan from the heat, uncover, and add the Pernod, orange zest, and the remaining 2 tablespoons olive oil, and shake the pan to combine. Remove and discard any mussels that have not opened. Taste and adjust the seasoning.

3. Divide the mussels and juices among 4 large, warmed bowls. Top each serving with a few grinds of pepper and serve with the bread triangles.

Roast Sturgeon with Cardoon and Chervil Sauce

SERVES 6 *Cardoons resemble large, wild heads of celery with lots of leaves on top. When cooked, this rather untidy-looking type of thistle has a flavor and texture that is a cross between celery and artichoke hearts. Sturgeon are best known for the eggs (caviar) that are harvested from certain species, but all sturgeon are good to eat. The meat is rich, dense, and mild. In the United States, some rivers in the Northwest have wild fisheries, and the fish are also being farmed in central California. Swordfish makes a good substitute in this recipe, though the texture is somewhat different.*

1 head cardoon, about 2 pounds

3 cups Fish Fumet (page 108) or reconstituted frozen fish stock

1 shallot, thinly sliced

1 garlic clove, thinly sliced

6 pieces skinless sturgeon fillet, 5 to 6 ounces each

Sea salt or kosher salt

Freshly ground pepper

1/2 cup plus 1 tablespoon extra virgin olive oil

1 cup packed fresh chervil sprigs

6 fresh chervil sprigs for garnish

1. Trim the base and tops from the cardoon stalks, leaving firm lower stalks 8 to 10 inches long. Peel away the strings from the backs of the stalks. Once trimmed, you should have about 3/4 pound.

2. Bring a large pot filled with salted water (2 table-spoons salt per quart of water) to a boil. Cut the cardoon stalks crosswise into slices 1/4 inch thick and plunge them immediately into the boiling water. Parboil until crisp tender, 10 to 15 minutes. Drain and shock in ice water. Reserve.

3. Preheat the oven to 475°F. Oil a large, rimmed baking sheet just large enough to hold the fish pieces without crowding.

continued

4. In a small saucepan, combine the fumet or stock, shallot, and garlic over high heat, bring to a boil, and boil until reduced to 2 cups, about 8 minutes. Strain through a fine-mesh sieve and keep warm.

5. Sprinkle both sides of the sturgeon pieces with salt and pepper and place them on the prepared pan. Pour the warm fumet around the fish. Roast the sturgeon until just opaque throughout when tested with a fork, about 7 minutes.

6. Meanwhile, in a sauté pan, heat 1 tablespoon olive oil over medium heat. Add the cardoon slices and sauté until heated through, about 3 minutes. Remove from the heat and season with salt and pepper. Divide the cardoon among 6 warmed dinner plates.

7. Place the sturgeon on top of the cardoon. Pour the liquid from the baking pan into a blender and add the 1 cup chervil sprigs. Process on high speed until puréed. Reduce the speed to medium and slowly pour in the $\frac{1}{2}$ cup olive oil in a thin, steady stream through the small hole in the center of the lid. Taste and adjust the seasoning. Strain the sauce through a fine-mesh sieve into a clean pitcher.

8. Pour the sauce around the fish on the plates. Garnish with the chervil sprigs and serve at once.

Pan-Seared Salmon with Olive Oil Emulsion Sauce

SERVES 6 *I first made this dish as a showcase for the flavors of our oil in midsummer, after it has started to mellow. Our West Coast king salmon has fattened up by this time, and makes a very rich and unctuous dish when combined with the sauce. The other flavors in the dish are restrained and allow the fish and olive oil to shine. One of the mellower oils from France or Liguria would also be a good choice here. This dish is complemented by roast tiny new potatoes and sautéed spinach or young green beans.*

2 shallots, thinly sliced

1 clove garlic

6 fennel seeds

3 peppercorns

1½ cups dry, fruity white wine

4 cups Fish Fumet (page 108) or reconstituted frozen fish stock

½ cup extra virgin olive oil, plus extra for cooking salmon

⅛ teaspoon sea salt or kosher salt, plus extra for sprinkling over fish

6 pieces skinless salmon fillet, 4 to 6 ounces each

Freshly ground pepper

1. In a 2-quart saucepan, combine the shallots, garlic, fennel seeds, peppercorns, and wine and reduce over medium heat until almost dry. This will take 10 to 15 minutes. Reduce the heat as the level of liquid in the pan becomes lower in order to lessen the chances of burning. Add the fumet or stock, increase the heat to high, and reduce the liquid to ¾ cup, about 10 minutes.

2. Pour the reduced fumet through a fine-mesh sieve into a blender, pressing down on the shallots to extract as much liquid as possible. With the motor running at medium speed, slowly pour in the olive oil in a thin, steady stream through the small hole in the center of the lid. Add ⅛ teaspoon salt, and taste and adjust the seasoning. Keep warm while preparing the salmon.

3. Sprinkle both sides of the salmon pieces with salt and pepper. Preheat 1 large or 2 medium sauté pans over high heat until a drop of water dances vigorously on the surface. Lightly coat the bottom of the pan(s) with olive oil and carefully add the salmon. Do not crowd the pan(s). Sear until a nice golden-brown crust forms on the undersides, 1 to 2 minutes. Turn over the salmon and sear on the second side for 3 minutes, reducing the heat to medium after 1 minute. Turn the salmon back to the first side and continue cooking until done to your liking.

4. If the sauce is too thick, add a little hot water to adjust the consistency. Place a pool of sauce in the center of each warmed dinner plate. Place the salmon on top of the sauce and serve at once.

Fish Fumet

MAKES ABOUT 3 QUARTS *Homemade fish fumet, or stock, will add extra richness to any recipe calling for fish stock. If you don't care to make your own, good-quality frozen concentrated fish stock bases are available in well-stocked supermarkets. However, I encourage you to try this quick and easy process at least once for its superior flavor.*

Fish bones, or frames, are available from any good fish market where the fishmongers cut their own fresh fish. These markets are often happy to get rid of the bones for little or nothing. If your fishmonger does not cut his or her own fish (some buy it precut), he or she can usually order bones from a regular supplier. You can use any nonoily fish with light-colored flesh. Halibut, sole, cod, and various rockfish are all good choices. If the gills and internal organs are still on the frames, ask your fishmonger to remove them before giving you the frames. A fumet must always remain at a simmer. If it boils, you will end up with a cloudy, strong-flavored stock.

2 leeks, about ¾ pound total weight, sliced ¼ inch thick, including pale green tops

1 yellow or white onion, about 6 ounces, sliced ¼ inch thick

2 celery stalks, sliced ¼ inch thick

2 cloves garlic

1 tablespoon extra virgin olive oil

4 pounds fresh fish frames (see recipe introduction)

1 cup dry white wine such as Sauvignon Blanc

4 quarts water

4 fresh flat-leaf parsley stems

3 fresh thyme sprigs

2 bay leaves

6 peppercorns

1. In a heavy, 6- to 8-quart pot, combine the leeks, onion, celery, garlic, and olive oil over low heat. Cover and sweat, stirring occasionally, until the vegetables are softened but not colored, 8 to 10 minutes.

2. Meanwhile, rinse the fish frames well in cold water. Using your fingers, remove the long, red strip of blood from along the cavity side of the backbone. Also, remove any remaining bits of internal organs and gills. Rinse the frames again in cold water. Using a cleaver or kitchen shears, cut the frames into pieces that will easily fit in your pot.

3. Add the fish frames to the vegetables and continue to sweat gently for 5 more minutes, stirring occasionally. Increase the heat to medium, add the wine, and cook for 2 minutes, stirring occasionally. Increase the heat to medium-high and add the water. Bring the water almost to a boil and then reduce the heat to low. Skim all of the foam and scum from the surface and discard. Add the parsley, thyme, bay leaves, and peppercorns and continue to cook for 30 minutes, skimming off any more scum that forms.

4. At the end of 30 minutes, turn off the heat and let the fumet rest, undisturbed, for 15 minutes. Pour the fumet through a colander into a clean, large bowl, leaving the last 1 or 2 cups containing the cloudy sediment behind. Strain the fumet once more, this time through a fine-mesh sieve or *chinois*. For a fumet that is sparkling clear, strain once more through a *chinois* lined with 4 layers of dampened cheesecloth. Use the fumet immediately, or chill and then freeze in small containers for up to 6 months.

Meats, Poultry, and Side Dishes

Most of us here at the ranch are unabashed carnivores. We enjoy our meat and poultry with a cornucopia of different vegetables from the kitchen garden, as well as fruit from the orchards, honey from the hives, and leaves off the trees.

The native California bay laurel offers a harvest of leaves that can be used, in moderation, to add a subtle, intriguing note to many dishes, including roast chicken (page 141). Select a free-range bird, add a fresh lemon or two, and you have some honest food that will stand any comparison.

When Brussels sprouts start forming like so many buttons on each long, thick stalk, Mark starts thinking about Braised Leg of Veal (page 126) with baby sprouts and creamy mashed potatoes. Another deliciously flavorful, lean meat is rabbit, which is popular in Europe but less so in the United States. If you have never tried it, I urge you to do so. Simply cooked with extra virgin olive oil, whole-grain mustard, and fresh thyme, as in the recipe on page 134, it's a revelation.

Also in this chapter you will find recipes for polenta (page 146) and two different but equally rewarding versions of Mashed Potatoes (page 144). They are included here because they are such natural partners with many of these meat and poultry dishes.

Spiced Pork Tenderloin with Cherries and Sweet Spices

SERVES 6 TO 8 *I first made this dish for an early summer lunch that was to be served on tables set out on the lawn. Bing cherries were ripening but there were not enough of them to make a dessert, so I decided to serve them as a garnish with the main course. You will need to plan ahead when making this recipe, as the pork must marinate for 1 to 3 days to absorb flavor from the spices. The roast potatoes included in Coriander-Crusted Pork Tenderloin with Roasted New Potatoes (page 114) make a perfect accompaniment.*

2 pork tenderloins, 1 pound each

1½ teaspoons peppercorns

½ teaspoon cardamom seeds

1 tablespoon ground ginger

½ teaspoon ground cinnamon

Pinch of red pepper flakes

3 cloves garlic, sliced

1 large shallot, sliced

4 tablespoons extra virgin olive oil

4 tablespoons port wine

2 teaspoons sea salt or kosher salt

¾ pound Bing or other flavorful dark red cherries, pitted

1 tablespoon red wine vinegar

½ teaspoon freshly ground pepper

1. Trim any silver skin from the pork tenderloins, as it toughens when cooked. In a small sauté pan, toast the peppercorns and cardamom seeds over medium-low heat until fragrant, about 5 minutes. Remove from the heat, let cool, then pour into a mortar. Add the ginger, cinnamon, and red pepper flakes and pound with a pestle to form a powder. Remove 1 tablespoon of the spice mixture and reserve for later use. Add the garlic and shallot to the mortar and continue pounding to form a paste. Pound in 1 tablespoon of the olive oil and 2 tablespoons of the port.

2. Put the pork and spice paste in a zippered heavy-duty plastic bag, expel all the air, and seal shut. Massage the bag to coat the pork evenly with the spice mixture. Place in the refrigerator and let marinate, turning occasionally, for 1 to 3 days. Remove from the refrigerator 1 hour before you begin cooking.

3. Preheat a 10-inch cast-iron skillet over high heat until a drop of water dances vigorously on the surface. Remove the tenderloins from the bag and sprinkle them with 1 1/2 teaspoons of the salt. Add 1 tablespoon of the olive oil to the hot pan and carefully add the pork. Brown the tenderloins on all sides, being careful not to scorch the spice paste. Reduce the heat to medium and continue cooking, turning often, until an instant-read thermometer inserted into the thickest part of each tenderloin registers 135°F (internal temperature will rise a few degrees as the meat rests), about 10 minutes. It should be a little pink inside and still juicy. Remove the tenderloins to a warmed platter and cover loosely with aluminum foil while cooking the cherries.

4. Preheat a sauté pan over high heat. Add the remaining 2 tablespoons olive oil and the cherries. Reduce the heat to medium and cook, shaking the pan often, for 30 seconds. Add the reserved 1 tablespoon spice mixture, the vinegar, the remaining 2 tablespoons port, the remaining 1/2 teaspoon salt, and the pepper. Increase the heat to high and cook, shaking the pan constantly, until the cherries have softened and the liquid has thickened slightly, about 3 minutes. If the cherries start to lose their shape, remove them from the pan while the liquid thickens. Remove from the heat.

5. Slice the meat on the diagonal and arrange on the warmed platter. Top with the cherries and their liquid and serve immediately.

VARIATION: *This dish can also be served as a main-course salad. Let the meat cool to room temperature before slicing. Remove the cherries from the pan and reduce the juices a little more. Use part of the reduced juices to fortify some Red Wine Vinaigrette (page 66). Dress lightly seasoned sturdy lettuces with the vinaigrette and arrange on chilled dinner plates. Slice the meat and arrange the slices on the lettuce leaves. Arrange the cherries on top and drizzle with the remaining reduced juices.*

Coriander-Crusted Pork Tenderloin with Roasted New Potatoes

SERVES 6 TO 8 *Pork tenderloin is a versatile cut that is low in fat, easy to cook, and has good texture. It is not, however, the most flavorful pork cut. Here, a richly spiced crust gives it a flavor boost and adds an aromatic crunchiness that heightens the flavor. My favorite potato for roasting this way is the Rose Finn.*

2 pork tenderloins, 1 pound each
1½ teaspoons peppercorns
3 tablespoons coriander seeds
3 cloves garlic
4 tablespoons extra virgin olive oil

1½ pounds new potatoes, unpeeled
2¼ teaspoons sea salt or kosher salt
½ teaspoon freshly ground pepper

1. Trim any silver skin from the pork tenderloins, as it toughens when cooked. In a small sauté pan, toast the peppercorns and coriander seeds over medium-low heat until fragrant, about 5 minutes. Remove from the heat, let cool, then pour into a mortar. Add the garlic and 1 tablespoon of the olive oil and pound with a pestle to form a coarse, moist paste. Put the pork and spice paste in a zippered heavy-duty plastic bag, expel all the air, and seal shut. Massage the bag to coat the pork evenly with the spice paste. Place in the refrigerator and let marinate, turning occasionally, for 1 to 3 days. Remove from the refrigerator 1 hour before you begin cooking.

2. Preheat the oven to 375°F. In a bowl, toss together the potatoes, ¾ teaspoon of the salt, the pepper, and 2 tablespoons of the olive oil until well coated. Pour into a shallow baking pan just large enough to hold the potatoes in a single layer. Place in the oven and roast, stirring occasionally, until tender when pierced with a fork, about 40 minutes.

3. About 20 minutes before the potatoes are ready, preheat a 10-inch cast-iron skillet over high heat. Remove the tenderloins from the bag and sprinkle them with the remaining 1½ teaspoons salt. Add the remaining 1 tablespoon olive oil to the hot pan, reduce the heat to medium, and carefully add the pork. Brown the tenderloins on all sides, being careful not to scorch the crust. Continue to cook, turning often, until an instant-read thermometer inserted into the thickest part of each tenderloin registers 135°F (internal temperature will rise a few degrees as the meat rests), about 10 minutes. It should be a little pink inside and still juicy. Remove the tenderloins to a warmed platter, cover loosely with aluminum foil, and let rest for 5 minutes.

4. Cut the tenderloins on the diagonal into slices ⅜ inch thick. Serve with the potatoes.

Spit-Roasted Pork Shoulder with Sage and Coriander

SERVES 12 *My favorite cut of pork is the shoulder. It is flavorful and has enough fat to stay tender and moist when cooked past medium-rare. It is the best choice for braising and for any long-cooked preparation. Sage and coriander are traditionally used with pork and here bring to mind American breakfast sausage. If you don't have a rotisserie, butterfly the meat and cook it flat on the grill for 15 to 20 minutes per side.*

1 pork shoulder, 5 to 6 pounds, boned
1 tablespoon peppercorns
1 tablespoon coriander seeds
2 cloves garlic, sliced
1 large shallot, sliced
1 tablespoon chopped fresh sage
2 tablespoons extra virgin olive oil
1½ teaspoons sea salt or kosher salt

1. Trim any large pieces of fat from the surface of the pork. In a small sauté pan, toast the peppercorns and coriander seeds over medium-low heat until fragrant, about 5 minutes. Remove from the heat, let cool, and pour into a mortar. Add the garlic, shallot, and sage and pound with a pestle to form a paste. Pound in the olive oil.

2. Put the pork and spice paste in a zippered heavy-duty plastic bag, expel all the air, and seal shut. Massage the bag to coat the pork evenly with the spice paste. Place in the refrigerator and let marinate, turning occasionally, for 2 to 3 days. Remove from the refrigerator 1 to 2 hours before you begin cooking.

3. Prepare a natural-charcoal fire in a grill and set up the rotisserie. Remove the pork from the bag, reserving the marinade. Thread the pork onto the rotisserie spindle and secure with clamps. Tie with butcher's twine as necessary to hold the pork in a compact mass well centered on the spindle and sprinkle evenly with the salt.

4. Cook the pork, following the rotisserie manufacturer's directions and basting after the first hour with the reserved marinade, until an instant-read thermometer inserted into the thickest part registers 150° to 160°F (the internal temperature will rise a few degrees as the meat rests) for juicy meat, about 1½ hours. (Due to variations in grills, rotisseries, and fires, it is impossible to give an exact time.) Place the meat on a warmed platter, cover lightly with aluminum foil, and let rest for 10 to 15 minutes before carving.

Spit-Roasted Pork Shoulder with Lavender, Honey, and Bay

SERVES 12 *I developed this recipe for one of our harvest parties to showcase some typical ranch flavors. We have extensive plantings of lavender, our bees make lavender honey, and we have both European bay trees and native California bay laurel trees. (The lavender, Lavandula angustifolia, used for cooking can be found dried at natural-foods stores; any kind of honey will do in the absence of lavender honey.) These flavors are just wonderful with spit-roasted pork. At the harvest party, we cook whole pigs on the rotisserie, but I have scaled down the recipe to make it more manageable. If you lack a rotisserie, you can butterfly the meat and cook it flat on a grill for 15 to 20 minutes on each side.*

1 pork shoulder, 5 to 6 pounds, boned

2 cloves garlic, sliced

1 shallot, sliced

1 tablespoon coarsely ground pepper

1½ tablespoons fresh lavender flowers (*Lavandula angustifolia*), or 2 tablespoons dried lavender flowers

3 bay leaves, preferably fresh, coarsely chopped

3 tablespoons extra virgin olive oil

2 tablespoons honey, preferably lavender

1 tablespoon cider vinegar

2 teaspoons sea salt or kosher salt

1. Trim any large pieces of fat from the surface of the pork. In a mortar using a pestle, pound together the garlic, shallot, pepper, lavender, and bay leaves until a paste forms. Add the olive oil, honey, and vinegar and continue pounding until well mixed.

2. Put the pork and spice paste in a zippered heavy-duty plastic bag, expel all the air, and seal shut. Massage the bag to coat the pork evenly with the spice paste. Place in the refrigerator and let marinate, turning occasionally, for 2 to 3 days. Remove from the refrigerator 1 to 2 hours before you begin cooking.

3. Prepare a natural-charcoal fire in a grill and set up the rotisserie. Remove the pork from the bag, reserving the marinade. Thread the pork onto the rotisserie spindle and secure with clamps. Tie with butcher's twine as necessary to hold the pork in a compact mass well centered on the spindle and sprinkle evenly with the salt.

4. Cook the pork, following the rotisserie manufacturer's directions and basting after the first hour with the reserved marinade, until an instant-read thermometer inserted into the thickest part of the pork registers 150° to 160°F (the internal temperature will rise a few degrees as the meat rests) for juicy meat, about 1½ hours. (Due to variations in grills, rotisseries, and fires, it is impossible to give an exact time.) Place the meat on a warmed platter, cover lightly with aluminum foil, and let rest for 10 to 15 minutes before carving.

Grilled Lamb Chops with Yogurt and Indian Spices

SERVES 4 *The produce that Margaret grows is so flavorful that I find myself using fewer seasonings than I have in the past. Occasionally, however, I like to spice things up. In India, cooks don't use "curry powder." Instead, they make a* masala, *or spice mixture, that is carefully adjusted according to the main ingredient and can range from subtle, like this one, to fiery hot. I like to serve these chops with Raita (page 68) and Herbed Cherry Tomato Salad (page 51) and with warmed pita bread and/or a rice pilaf.*

spice mixture

1 tablespoon peppercorns

1 tablespoon cumin seeds

1 tablespoon coriander seeds

1 teaspoon cardamom seeds (removed from husks)

1 teaspoon small cinnamon stick pieces

¾ teaspoon ground turmeric

1 teaspoon paprika

½ teaspoon red pepper flakes

1½ teaspoons ground ginger

lamb

1 large clove garlic, sliced

1 shallot, sliced

2 teaspoons spice mixture (above)

2 teaspoons extra virgin olive oil

¼ cup plain yogurt

2 teaspoons grated lemon zest

1 tablespoon fresh lemon juice

8 lamb rib chops, each 1¼ inches thick, frenched (see note, page 120)

¾ teaspoon sea salt or kosher salt

eggplants

6 small Japanese eggplants, each about 5 inches long

1 tablespoon reserved spice mixture (above)

2 tablespoons extra virgin olive oil

¾ teaspoon sea salt or kosher salt

1. To prepare the spice mixture, in a small sauté pan, toast the peppercorns, cumin, coriander, cardamom, and cinnamon over medium-low heat until the cumin seeds begin to darken and the mixture is very fragrant, 4 to 5 minutes. Remove from the heat, let cool, and pour into a mortar. Add the turmeric, paprika, red pepper flakes, and ginger and pound with a pestle to a coarse powder. (Alternatively, grind the spices in an electric spice grinder.) Measure out 1 tablespoon plus 2 teaspoons of the spice mixture to use for the recipe. Store the remainder in a covered jar in a cool, dark place to use another time.

continued

2. To prepare the lamb, in a mortar using a pestle, pound together the garlic, shallot, spice mixture, and olive oil until a rough paste forms. Stir in the yogurt, lemon zest, and lemon juice. Rub the paste onto the lamb chops, coating them on both sides, and allow the meat to rest, covered, at room temperature for at least 1 1/2 hours, or in the refrigerator for up to 24 hours. If refrigerated, bring the meat to room temperature before cooking.

3. Prepare a hot natural-charcoal fire in a grill.

4. To prepare the eggplants, trim off the stem end from each eggplant, then cut in half lengthwise. Use a long knife and cut as straight as possible so that the eggplant halves will lie flat on the grill. Using a sharp paring knife, make a pattern of crosshatch cuts about 1/4 inch apart on the cut surface of each eggplant half. The cuts should reach almost to the skin without piercing it. Using your fingers, rub about 1/4 teaspoon of the spice mixture into the cuts on each eggplant half. Just before grilling, brush the cut sides with the olive oil and sprinkle with the salt.

5. To grill the lamb chops and eggplants, scrape off the excess marinade from the chops and season them with the salt. Place the eggplants over the fire and grill, turning them several times, until they are dark golden brown on the cut sides and are soft throughout, about 10 minutes in all. Grill the chops at the same time for about 4 minutes on each side for medium-rare, or to the desired degree of doneness.

6. To serve, place 2 lamb chops and 3 eggplant halves on each of 4 warmed dinner plates and serve at once.

NOTE: *To "french" a lamb chop means to scrape the bone clean of all fat and gristle down as far as the tender little nut of meat, or only halfway down if you prefer. You can ask your butcher to do it, or you can do it yourself using a small knife with a thin, rigid blade.*

Grasp the chop by the meat end and hold it about 3 inches above a cutting board, with the tip of the bone resting on the board to steady the chop. Using the back of the knife blade, scrape the bone to remove any remaining fat and tissue, turning the chop as you go to clean all sides.

Grilled Lamb Chops with Red Onion Marmalade and Celery Root Purée

SERVES 4 *One of the joys of late fall at the ranch are the fantastic celery roots that Margaret harvests from her vegetable garden. This recipe pairs a purée of these knobby roots, also known as celeriac, with savory lamb chops made aromatic and slightly sweet from the addition of lavender and pomegranate molasses. The red onion marmalade served alongside adds a tart-sweet note to balance the richness of the meat. If you have an immersion blender, you can use it to finish the purée. It will make it creamier and seem richer, even though it is low in calories. Look for pomegranate molasses in Middle Eastern and some natural-foods stores. We often cook lamb chops in our wood-burning oven. The smoke and extra heat from the fire caramelizes the surface of the meat and gives it a nice, smoky aroma without charring it.*

lamb

1 clove garlic, sliced

1 shallot, sliced

½ teaspoon peppercorns

½ teaspoon dried lavender flowers (*Lavandula angustifolia*)

2 teaspoons extra virgin olive oil

1 tablespoon pomegranate molasses

8 lamb rib chops, each 1¼ inches thick, frenched (see note, page 120)

¾ teaspoon sea salt or kosher salt

red onion marmalade

2 red onions, sliced ⅛ inch thick

1 teaspoon sea salt or kosher salt

½ teaspoon freshly ground pepper

2 tablespoons extra virgin olive oil

2 tablespoons balsamic vinegar

1 tablespoon red wine vinegar

celery root purée

1 celery root, about 1½ pounds, peeled and cut into rough chunks

2 cups whole milk

½ teaspoon sea salt or kosher salt

¼ teaspoon freshly ground pepper

1 tablespoon extra virgin olive oil

Pomegranate seeds for garnish (optional)

1. To prepare the lamb, in a mortar using a pestle, pound together the garlic, shallot, peppercorns, lavender, olive oil, and pomegranate molasses until a rough paste forms. Rub the paste onto the lamb chops, coating them on both sides, and allow the meat to rest, covered, at room temperature for 1½ hours, or in the refrigerator for up to 24 hours. If refrigerated, bring the meat to room temperature before cooking.

continued

2. To prepare the onion marmalade, combine the onions, salt, pepper, and olive oil in a heavy sauté pan over medium heat. Cook, stirring frequently, until the onions begin to soften, about 5 minutes. Add the balsamic vinegar and the red wine vinegar and stir to combine. Cover the surface of the onions with a circle of baking parchment cut to fit the pan, and then cover the pan with a tight-fitting lid. Reduce the heat to very low and allow to cook undisturbed for 1 hour. Taste and adjust the seasoning; keep warm.

3. To prepare the celery root purée, in a saucepan, combine the celery root and milk over medium heat and bring to a simmer. Reduce the heat to maintain a simmer, cover partially, and cook slowly until the celery root is tender, about 30 minutes. Using a slotted spoon, remove the celery root from the pan, reserving the cooking liquid, and pass it through the fine screen of a food mill placed over a bowl, or push it through a coarse-mesh sieve with a wooden spoon. Beat in the salt, pepper, and olive oil. Use leftover cooking liquid as necessary to adjust consistency. Taste and adjust the seasoning; keep warm.

4. While the celery root is cooking, prepare a hot natural-charcoal fire in a grill.

5. To grill the lamb chops, scrape off the excess marinade and season them with the salt. Place the chops over the charcoal fire and grill for about 4 minutes on each side for medium-rare, or to the desired degree of doneness.

6. To serve, mound one-fourth of the celery root purée in the center of each of 4 warmed dinner plates. Lean 2 chops against each mound and put one-fourth of the onion marmalade on each plate. Garnish with a few pomegranate seeds (if using) and serve at once.

Braised Leg of Veal

SERVES 8 TO 10 *To make this dish, select a boned, rolled, and tied leg of veal. The meat practically falls apart, but because the veal stays half submerged in vegetables and stock during its three-hour cooking time, it stays moist and tender. It goes beautifully with tender, young Brussels sprouts and mashed potatoes.*

1 boneless leg of veal, about 4 pounds, rolled and tied

2 teaspoons sea salt or kosher salt

1 teaspoon freshly ground pepper

½ bunch celery, plus 1 stalk

3 carrots, peeled

1 large yellow onion, halved

5 tablespoons extra virgin olive oil

3 cloves garlic, chopped

¾ cup dry red wine

4 cups homemade veal stock or reconstituted frozen veal stock

5 fresh thyme sprigs

About 6 tablespoons Madeira wine

Double recipe Mashed Potatoes (page 145) for serving

2 pounds young Brussels sprouts, boiled in salted water until crisp tender, drained, and kept warm, for serving

1. Preheat the oven to 325°F. Season the leg of veal with the salt and pepper and set it aside. Chop the ½ bunch celery, 2 of the carrots, and half of the onion into large dice. Set aside.

2. Preheat a heavy, 6-quart Dutch oven over medium-high heat. Add 2 tablespoons of the olive oil and the veal and brown on all sides. Remove the veal from the pot. Take the pot off the heat and wipe out any remaining oil with a paper towel, being careful not to scrape out any of the browned bits of veal stuck to the bottom (the *fond*). Put the pot back on the burner, reduce the heat to medium-low, and add 2 tablespoons of the olive oil. Add the chopped vegetables and stir with a wooden spoon until the vegetables just start to soften, about 5 minutes. Add the garlic and as soon as you can smell it, add ½ cup of the red wine and increase the heat to medium. Reduce the wine until the pot is almost dry, stirring with a wooden spoon to scrape up the browned bits. Add 3 cups of the veal stock, bring to a simmer, and return the veal to the pot. Add 2 of the thyme sprigs, cover, place in the oven, and braise for 3 hours. Turn the veal every hour, and make sure that it is always at least half submerged. If at any time the level of liquid is less than that, add a little water.

3. To prepare the sauce, finely dice the remaining celery stalk, carrot, and onion half. Preheat a small saucepan over medium heat. Add the remaining 1 tablespoon olive oil and the finely diced vegetables and sauté until the onion starts to become translucent, about 5 minutes. Add the remaining 1/4 cup red wine and about half of the Madeira and reduce until the pan is almost dry. Add the remaining 1 cup veal stock and 3 thyme sprigs and bring the mixture to a simmer, skimming off the scum that rises to the top with a ladle or a small spoon. Cook gently until reduced by half, about 15 minutes, continuing to skim any impurities from the surface. Strain the sauce through a fine-mesh sieve into a clean pan and taste and adjust the seasoning, adding more Madeira wine to taste. Reheat gently just before serving.

4. To serve, remove the veal from the pot, discard the string, and cut the veal into slices or chunks. (Strain the cooking liquid and save for another use. It will keep, tightly covered and refrigerated, for 5 days, or may be frozen for up to 6 months.) Divide the mashed potatoes among warmed dinner plates. Divide the cut veal and place it on the mashed potatoes. Ladle the sauce on top of the meat and the potatoes. Arrange the Brussels sprouts on the plates and serve immediately.

Braised Short Ribs

SERVES 4 *Short ribs are one of the most flavorful cuts of beef, but they require long, slow braising to become tender. During this time, the meat takes on flavor from the wine and vegetables while the braising liquid becomes enriched with meat juices. If you have saved the braising liquid from Braised Leg of Veal (page 126), add ½ cup of it along with the wine. I have included a small amount of red wine vinegar, which helps to tenderize the meat while adding flavor to the sauce. Serve the ribs with rice or with Potato Purée (page 145).*

3 pounds beef short ribs, cut into 3- or 4-inch lengths

¾ teaspoon sea salt or kosher salt

½ teaspoon freshly ground pepper

2 tablespoons extra virgin olive oil

1 small head garlic, separated into cloves and peeled

1 small carrot, peeled and cut into chunks

1 yellow onion, cut into chunks

1 red bell pepper, stemmed, seeded, and cut into chunks

4 plum tomatoes, about 10 ounces total weight, cut into chunks

1 tablespoon red wine vinegar

½ cup full-bodied red wine such as Zinfandel

⅛ teaspoon red pepper flakes

1 tablespoon fresh herb leaves such as thyme, oregano, or winter savory

1. Preheat a heavy, 4-quart Dutch oven over medium-high heat. Sprinkle the ribs all over with the salt and pepper. When the pot is hot, add 1 tablespoon of the olive oil and some of the ribs. Do not crowd the ribs in the pan, or they will steam instead of brown. Brown the ribs on all sides (including the ends), reducing the heat if necessary to keep them from overbrowning. Remove to a plate and repeat with the remaining ribs. When all of the ribs are browned, pour off the accumulated fat and discard it.

2. Add the remaining 1 tablespoon oil and the garlic, carrot, onion, and bell pepper to the pot over medium-high heat and cook, stirring often, until the vegetables are softened and beginning to brown, 6 to 7 minutes. Add the tomatoes and

vinegar and cook for another minute, stirring constantly. Reduce the heat to medium, return the ribs to the pot, and add the wine, pepper flakes, and herb. Using tongs, push the ribs down into the pot so that they are as covered as possible with the vegetables. Allow the mixture to come to a boil, cover the pot, and reduce the heat to maintain a gentle simmer. Cook, turning the ribs every hour or so, until they are tender and easily pierced with a fork, 2 1/2 to 3 1/2 hours.

3. When the ribs are done, remove them to a warmed platter and keep warm. Skim off and discard any fat from the surface of the cooking liquid, and transfer the contents of the pot to a blender. Process until well puréed, and then pass the sauce through a medium-mesh sieve or the medium screen of a food mill into a warmed bowl. Taste and adjust the seasoning.

4. Serve the ribs immediately, and pass the sauce at the table.

Grilled Flank Steak Salad

SERVES 4 OR 5 *Flank steak is a flavorful, but tough, cut of beef. In the short rib recipe (page 128), the toughness is broken down by long cooking. In this recipe, the toughness is minimized by short cooking and by thinly slicing the meat. Use inexpensive bulk balsamic vinegar in the marinade, and save your better-quality balsamic vinegar (one that has been aged for at least 2 years) for the vinaigrette.*

1 large shallot, thinly sliced

2 cloves garlic, thinly sliced

1 tablespoon fresh oregano leaves, or 1½ teaspoons dried oregano

2 tablespoons extra virgin olive oil, plus 1 tablespoon if using a skillet

1 tablespoon inexpensive balsamic vinegar (see recipe introduction)

1¾ teaspoons freshly ground pepper

1 flank steak, about 1½ pounds

balsamic vinaigrette

1 large shallot, finely chopped

½ cup extra virgin olive oil

½ teaspoon sea salt or kosher salt

½ teaspoon freshly ground pepper

2 tablespoons moderate-quality balsamic vinegar (see recipe introduction)

2 tablespoons red wine vinegar

1 large red onion, cut into ¼-inch-wide strips

1¼ teaspoons sea salt or kosher salt

2 large red bell peppers, roasted and peeled, then cut lengthwise into strips (page 132)

6 ounces *haricots verts*, blanched for 1 minute in boiling water, drained, and shocked in ice water

6 ounces sturdy salad greens such as romaine

1 tablespoon balsamic syrup (see note)

1. On a cutting board using a large chef's knife, finely chop together the shallot, garlic, and fresh oregano. (If using dried oregano, crumble and add along with the pepper.) Scrape the chopped mixture into a nonreactive container large enough to hold the flank steak. Mix in the olive oil, vinegar, and 1 teaspoon of the pepper. Add the flank steak and turn to coat with the marinade. Cover and set aside to marinate for 2 hours at room temperature, or in the refrigerator for up to 24 hours. If refrigerated, bring the meat to room temperature before cooking.

2. To prepare the vinaigrette, in a small bowl, whisk together all the ingredients. Taste and adjust the seasoning.

3. Put the onion strips in a medium-sized bowl, add 2 tablespoons of the vinaigrette, $1/4$ teaspoon of the salt, and $1/4$ teaspoon of the pepper. Toss to coat and set aside.

4. Prepare a hot natural-charcoal fire in a grill, or preheat a large cast-iron skillet over high heat. Remove the steak from marinade and scrape off the excess marinade. Using the remaining $1/2$ teaspoon pepper and $1/2$ teaspoon of the salt, season the steak on both sides. Place the steak over the hot charcoal fire and grill, turning once, until an instant-read thermometer inserted in the thickest part registers 125°F for medium-rare, 3 to 4 minutes on each side. If using a skillet, film the pan with an additional 1 tablespoon olive oil and cook, turning once, for 4 to 5 minutes on each side for medium-rare, reducing the heat if necessary to prevent overbrowning. Transfer to a cutting board, cover lightly with aluminum foil, and let rest for 5 to 10 minutes while you finish the salad.

5. Preheat a sauté pan over medium-high heat. Add the onion strips and their marinade and sauté quickly until the onion begins to color and just starts to soften, about 3 minutes. Return them to their bowl. Add the roasted peppers, *haricots verts*, $1/4$ teaspoon of the salt, and 2 tablespoons of the vinaigrette to the bowl and toss to combine. Taste and adjust the seasoning. Put the lettuce in a large bowl and toss with the remaining $1/4$ teaspoon salt and the remaining vinaigrette. Taste and adjust the seasoning.

6. Divide the lettuce among 4 or 5 dinner plates. Using a long, sharp knife, thinly slice the meat across the grain. Divide the meat evenly among the plates, arranging the slices so that they partially overlap the lettuce. Divide the sautéed vegetable mixture evenly among the plates, placing it so that it partially overlaps the meat. Drizzle the salads with the balsamic syrup.

NOTE: *Balsamic syrup is a dynamic and inexpensive flavor enhancer easily made by reducing inexpensive bulk balsamic vinegar by half (or a little more) in a nonreactive saucepan over high heat. It is particularly useful with grilled meats and vegetables. The syrup keeps well refrigerated. We keep some on hand in a small, plastic squeeze bottle.*

Roasting Bell Peppers

Peppers of all types have a tough outer membrane. In some cases, it is desirable to remove this membrane, or skin, to improve the taste and texture of a dish. This is done by using heat to char and blister the membrane, making it easy to remove. You can rub the peppers with a light coat of oil, put them into a hot (500°F) oven, and turn them occasionally until the skin is blistered on all sides. You can also roast them on a gas-stove burner. Just put them, 1 or 2 at a time, directly on the grate over a burner turned on high. Use tongs to turn the peppers frequently until they are evenly blistered. My favorite method is to roast them on the grill over a hot charcoal fire, which adds a nice smoky flavor. If your grill rack is adjustable, position it close to the fire and put the peppers directly on it. Again, use tongs to turn the peppers until they are evenly blistered.

Whichever roasting method you use, place the hot blistered peppers in a plastic bag or a bowl, close the bag or cover the bowl, and allow the peppers to steam until cool. This step helps loosen the skin, making it easier to remove. When cool, transfer the peppers, one at a time, to a cutting board. Use your fingers to remove as much of the papery skin as possible. Keep a bowl of water nearby and dip your fingers into it to remove the bits of charred skin that stick to them. Never rinse the peppers themselves, as I feel this removes some of their flavor. When all the easily removed skin is gone, remove the stem, seeds, and ribs. I like to do this on a cutting board, using a bench scraper to cut off the top, slit the pepper open, and scrape out the seeds and ribs. Then I pick up the pepper with one hand, scrape the cutting board clean with the bench scraper, lay the pepper back down, skin side up, and remove the remaining skin with a few more swipes of the scraper.

Rabbit Two Ways with Grainy Mustard Sauce

SERVES 4 *Rabbit is a flavorful, lean meat that takes well to marinades. A young fryer rabbit is tender enough to cook quickly on the grill or the stove, but will also stand up to braising. In this recipe, I have grilled the leaner loins and braised the hind legs and the front leg and shoulder portions in their marinade. The braising liquid is then made into a sauce for the dish. You will need to start by marinating the rabbit 24 to 36 hours before you plan to serve it. I like to accompany the rabbit with Polenta (page 146), but it is also good with Potato Purée (page 145).*

2 shallots, chopped

1 large clove garlic, chopped

1 teaspoon chopped fresh thyme

2 ½ teaspoons freshly ground pepper

4 tablespoons extra virgin olive oil

4 tablespoons whole-grain Dijon mustard

2 fryer rabbits, about 5 pounds total weight, each cut into 2 hind leg portions, 2 loin portions, and 2 front leg and shoulder portions (reserve kidneys and livers for another use)

2 yellow onions, about 1 pound total weight, sliced

1 ¼ teaspoons sea salt or kosher salt

1 cup dry white wine

1 ½ tablespoons crème fraîche or heavy cream

Polenta (page 146) for serving

Chopped fresh thyme for garnish

1. Using a mortar and pestle or a mini chopper, reduce the shallots, garlic, 1 teaspoon thyme, 2 teaspoons of the pepper, 2 tablespoons of the olive oil, and 2 tablespoons of the mustard to a rough paste. Put the rabbit pieces and the paste in a zippered heavy-duty plastic bag, expel all the air, and seal shut. Massage the bag to coat the rabbit pieces evenly with the paste. Place in the refrigerator and let marinate, turning occasionally, for 24 to 36 hours. Remove from the refrigerator 1 hour before you begin cooking.

2. Preheat a large sauté pan over high heat. Add 1 ½ teaspoons of the olive oil to the pan and a few of the rabbit leg portions. Take care not to crowd the pan, or they will steam instead of brown. Reduce the heat slightly and sear the rabbit pieces, turning them to brown on all sides. When each piece is browned, remove it to a side plate and repeat until all the rabbit leg portions are browned.

3. Add 1 tablespoon of the olive oil, the onions, and 3/4 teaspoon of the salt to the pan, reduce the heat to medium, and cook, stirring often, until the onions soften and the browned bits come free from the bottom of the pan, about 5 minutes. Add the wine and 1 tablespoon of the remaining mustard. Increase the heat to high and bring the mixture to a boil, stirring occasionally. Return the rabbit pieces to the pan and reduce the heat to medium-low. Cover and allow the meat to braise for 1 hour, turning the pieces every 15 minutes. Adjust the heat as necessary to maintain a simmer.

4. Prepare a hot natural-charcoal fire in a grill, or preheat a large sauté pan over high heat. Season the rabbit loin sections with the remaining 1/2 teaspoon each salt and pepper. Brown them on the grill or in the sauté pan on the stove top. If cooking on the grill, place directly over the fire and grill, turning as needed, until browned on all sides. Then move the loin sections away from the direct heat and continue cooking, turning frequently, until medium-rare, about 15 minutes. If cooking on the stove top, pour enough olive oil into the hot pan to film the bottom and then sear the loin pieces on both sides. Reduce the heat to medium and continue cooking, turning once, until medium-rare, 10 to 12 minutes. Alternatively, after browning, slide the sauté pan (be sure it is oven-proof) into a 375°F oven for 8 to 10 minutes.

5. While the loins are cooking, remove the rabbit leg portions from the braising pan and keep warm. Pour the contents of the pan into a blender and add the remaining 1 tablespoon mustard and the crème fraîche or cream. Process until smooth. If the consistency is too thick, add a little hot water. Taste and adjust the seasoning. Transfer to a warmed bowl, and keep warm.

6. To serve, place 1 loin portion, 1 front leg, and 1 hind leg portion on each warmed dinner plate. Add a mound of polenta, and ladle the sauce on top of the rabbit and the polenta. Garnish with thyme.

Cinnamon-Rubbed Duck Breast with Grilled Prosciutto-Wrapped Peaches

SERVES 4 *This is a spectacular summer dish and, like the peach-topped focaccia (page 92), it gives us a good excuse to eat tree-ripened peaches during their brief season. The chewy saltiness of the grilled prosciutto is a great complement to the delicate sweetness of the fruit. Buy the largest duck breasts that you can find. Larger breasts are meatier in proportion to the skin and fat, and the meat is more flavorful. Do not remove the skin before cooking, as the fat protects the meat and adds a great deal of flavor during cooking. If a guest is concerned about eating the fat (the meat itself is low in fat), the skin is easily removed at the table.*

2 boneless whole duck breasts, about 1 pound each
1 teaspoon freshly ground pepper
1 teaspoon ground cinnamon
1 tablespoon extra virgin olive oil
¾ teaspoon sea salt or kosher salt

peaches

2 firm but ripe peaches, about 6 ounces each
2 slices prosciutto, not too thin
2 teaspoons extra virgin olive oil
Sea salt or kosher salt
Freshly ground pepper

sauce

2 tablespoons brandy
1 tablespoon fresh lemon juice
4 cups chicken or duck stock, boiled to reduce
   to 1 cup and kept warm
2 tablespoons unsalted butter
Sea salt or kosher salt
Freshly ground pepper

1. Working from the meat side, separate the halves of the breast by cutting on either side of the strip of cartilage that remains from the breastbone. Trim off any fat and skin that projects beyond the meat. Turn the halves skin side up. Using a sharp, thin knife, cut a crosshatch pattern of slits about ½ inch apart in the skin and fat. The cuts should extend almost to the meat without actually reaching it. Combine the pepper and cinnamon and rub it into both sides of the breasts. Put the meat and the olive oil in a zippered heavy-duty plastic bag, expel all the air, and seal shut. Massage the bag to coat the duck evenly with the oil and spices. Place in the refrigerator and let marinate, turning occasionally, for at least 4 hours or for up to 36 hours. Remove from the refrigerator 1 hour before you begin cooking.

2. To prepare the peaches, bring a large saucepan filled with water to a boil, add the peaches, and blanch for 30 seconds, or just until the skins begin to loosen. Drain the peaches, plunge them into ice

continued

water until cool, and then peel. Cut each peach into 6 wedges, discarding the pit. Cut the prosciutto slices in half lengthwise to form 4 long, narrow strips. Work with 3 peach wedges and 1 prosciutto strip at a time. Arrange the 3 peach wedges side by side on a work surface and snake the prosciutto strip between them in a figure-8 fashion, making sure that the prosciutto covers as much of the peach surface as possible. Thread a bamboo skewer through the wedges, securing the prosciutto in place. Repeat with 3 more peach wedges and 1 prosciutto strip and slide them onto the same skewer. Repeat with remaining peaches and prosciutto, loading a second skewer. Pour the olive oil on a plate, place the skewers on the plate, and turn to coat on all sides with the oil. Season lightly with salt and pepper. Reserve.

3. Prepare a hot natural-charcoal fire in a grill, and preheat a heavy sauté pan over high heat on the stove top. Season the duck breast halves on both sides with the salt and place them, skin side down, in the hot pan. Reduce the heat slightly and brown the breasts. As the fat renders out of the skin, pour it off into a heatproof container. If the skin is browning too fast, reduce the heat a little more. You are trying to render as much fat as possible from the skin while forming a

crispy brown crust. When the skin side is done to your liking, increase the heat again and brown the meat side for about 3 minutes. Do not overcook. Duck breast tastes best when served rare or medium-rare. When done to your liking, remove from the pan and keep warm.

4. To prepare the sauce, pour off any remaining fat and return the pan to low heat. Add the brandy and lemon juice and deglaze the pan, stirring to scrape up any browned bits. Add the hot reduced stock to the pan, increase the heat to medium, and boil until reduced to about 1/2 cup, about 4 minutes. Whisk in the butter, and season with salt and pepper; keep warm.

5. Meanwhile, place the peach skewers over the charcoal fire and grill, turning once, until the prosciutto is crisp and golden brown, about 3 minutes on each side. (I know it seems like a lot of trouble to light the grill just for the peaches, but they are really good.)

6. To serve, carve the duck breast halves on the diagonal into slices 3/8 inch thick. Fan the slices out on warmed dinner plates. Slide the peaches off the skewers and place one group of the peaches on each plate. Spoon the sauce over the duck breast slices and serve at once.

Roast Lemon-Bay Chicken

SERVES 4 *This is a simple dish in which the acidity of the lemon, the aromatic pungency of the bay leaves, and the bite of the black pepper work together to complement the rich flavor of the chicken. I like to use the leaves of the native California bay laurel, but there is no reason why you cannot use the Mediterranean, or true bay. Serve with Potato Purée (page 145) or Polenta (page 146) and spinach sautéed in olive oil.*

1 fryer chicken, preferably free range, 3 to 4 pounds
2 lemons
20 fresh California bay leaves
2 tablespoons extra virgin olive oil
2 teaspoons coarsely ground pepper
1 teaspoon sea or kosher salt

1. Remove the giblets from the cavity of the chicken and reserve for another use. Rinse the chicken inside and out and then pat dry. Place the chicken in a bowl or in a zippered heavy-duty plastic bag. Using your palm, roll the lemons back and forth on a countertop to free their juice, then quarter them lengthwise. Place the lemon quarters, bay leaves, olive oil, and pepper in the bowl or bag. If using the bowl, turn the chicken to coat evenly and cover the bowl. If using the bag, expel the air, seal shut, and massage the bag to coat the chicken with the seasonings. Place in the refrigerator and let marinate, turning once or twice, for at least 12 hours or for up to 36 hours. Remove from the refrigerator 1 hour before you begin cooking.

2. Preheat the oven to 425°F. Remove the chicken from the bowl or bag, and reserve the marinade. Rub ½ teaspoon of the salt in the cavity and add half of the bay leaves and as many of the lemon quarters as will fit. Rub the outside of the chicken with the remaining ½ teaspoon of salt. Place the chicken, breast side down, on a rack in a shallow roasting pan.

3. Roast for 30 minutes. Squeeze the juice from the remaining lemon quarters and add it to the reserved marinade. After another 20 minutes, baste with the reserved marinade and the pan juices. Turn the chicken breast side up and continue roasting for 20 to 30 minutes longer, basting several times with the accumulated pan juices and any remaining marinade. The chicken is done when an instant-read thermometer inserted into the thickest part of the thigh away from the bone registers 165°F, or the juices run clear when a thigh joint is pierced.

4. Remove the chicken to a warmed platter and cover lightly with aluminum foil. Let rest in a warm place for 15 minutes before carving. Strain the pan juices and any juices that have accumulated on the platter through a fine-mesh sieve placed over a small saucepan, and spoon off some of the fat if desired. Bring the liquid to a boil. Taste and adjust the seasoning. Pour into a warmed bowl or sauceboat.

5. To serve, carve the chicken and divide among warmed dinner plates. Pass the pan juices at the table.

Chicken Thighs Stuffed with Mushrooms and Herbs

SERVES 4 *To me, this is a wonderful example of comfort food. The rich meatiness of the chicken combines well with the woodsy flavor of the mushroom stuffing. When served with a succulent accompaniment of sautéed greens, the chicken really needs no sauce other than a drizzle of extra virgin olive oil.*

4 large chicken thighs, 6 to 8 ounces each, boned
   with skin intact
3 tablespoons extra virgin olive oil
½ pound fresh cremini or white mushrooms,
   thinly sliced
¾ teaspoon sea salt or kosher salt, plus more
   for seasoning
1 slice pancetta (about 1 ounce), cut into small dice
1 yellow onion, cut into small dice (about ¾ cup)
1 shallot, chopped
1 tablespoon dried porcini mushroom pieces, soaked
   in very hot water to cover for 10 minutes
1 clove garlic, finely chopped
½ teaspoon freshly ground pepper, plus more
   for seasoning
2 tablespoons chopped fresh herbs such as oregano,
   sage, parsley, and/or thyme
1 tablespoon freshly grated Parmigiano-Reggiano
   cheese
¼ cup shredded mozzarella cheese
1 cup fresh white bread crumbs, made from day-old
   country-style bread

sautéed greens

2 tablespoons extra virgin olive oil
1 large bunch Swiss chard, beet greens, or kale,
   stems removed and leaves chopped
½ teaspoon sea salt or kosher salt
Pinch of red pepper flakes

Extra virgin olive oil for serving

1. Using a sharp, narrow-bladed knife, remove any bits of bone or cartilage remaining on the chicken thighs.

2. To prepare the stuffing, preheat a large sauté pan over high heat. Add 1½ teaspoons of the olive oil and then add half of the sliced fresh mushrooms. Cook, stirring constantly, until the mushrooms begin to color, about 1½ minutes. Sprinkle with ¼ teaspoon salt and continue cooking until any moisture the mushrooms have given off has evaporated, about 1 minute longer. Remove the cooked mushrooms to a bowl, wipe the pan out, and repeat with another 1½ teaspoons olive oil, the remaining mushrooms, and ¼ teaspoon salt. Set the mushrooms aside.

3. In a medium sauté pan, cook the pancetta over medium heat, stirring occasionally, until it starts to color, about 5 minutes. Discard any accumulated fat. Add 1 tablespoon of the oil, the onions, and the shallot to the pancetta and continue cooking, stirring often, until the onion softens, about 5 minutes. Remove the porcini from their soaking liquid, reserving the liquid, and chop them roughly. Add the porcini, their liquid, garlic, $1/4$ teaspoon salt, and $1/2$ teaspoon pepper to the onion mixture and cook until aromatic, another 2 minutes. Add to the bowl with the mushrooms along with the herbs, both cheeses, and the bread crumbs. Stir to combine, then taste and adjust the seasoning.

4. Preheat the oven to 350°F. Place the chicken thighs, meat side up and with a short side facing you, on a work surface. Place one-fourth of the stuffing mixture in a horizontal line at the center of each thigh. Starting from the short side nearest you, roll up each thigh and secure with a bamboo skewer. (Think of returning each piece to its original form with a cylinder of stuffing in place of the bone.) Season the outsides of the rolls lightly with salt and pepper.

5. Return the large sauté pan to medium-high heat and add the remaining 1 tablespoon olive oil. Add the chicken rolls and brown on all sides, about 5 minutes. Transfer the thighs to a shallow baking pan and bake until cooked through when tested with a knife, about 15 minutes.

6. While the thighs are baking, prepare the greens: Rinse out the large sauté pan and preheat it over high heat. Add the olive oil and the greens and cook, stirring constantly with tongs or a wooden spoon, until the greens have broken down and rendered their moisture into the pan, 3 to 5 minutes. Reduce the heat slightly and add the salt and red pepper flakes. Continue cooking, stirring often, until the liquid has evaporated, just a few minutes. Remove from the heat and keep warm.

7. Remove the thighs to a cutting board and let rest for a few minutes. Remove the skewers and slice each thigh on the diagonal into 4 or 5 slices. Divide the greens among 4 warmed dinner plates. Fan the thigh slices over the greens, and drizzle with a little olive oil. Serve immediately.

Mashed Potatoes and Potato Purée

There are many variations on the mashed potato theme, and this much-loved side dish is not an exclusively American favorite. In preparing all mashed potato recipes, the constants are cooked potatoes combined with liquid, fat, and seasonings. There can be, however, variation in the type of potatoes used and the method used for cooking them, as well as the quantity and nature of the other ingredients.

In Mark's Mashed Potatoes recipe, the liquid is milk, the fat is butter, and the seasonings are salt and white pepper. If you would like to make a decadently rich version, bake russet potatoes instead of boiling them (to decrease the amount of moisture they contain, thus making room for more added liquid), put them through the medium screen of a food mill, substitute cream for the milk, and increase the amount of butter. Experiment with the exact proportions until you find a ratio that you like. A good starting point would be 3 parts cream to 1 part butter. If you have ever had mashed potatoes in a fine restaurant and could not believe how good they were, extra butter and cream is the probable reason. For a change of pace, the liquid in my Potato Purée recipe is a mixture of the potato cooking liquid and milk. The fat is olive oil, and the seasoning is simply the salt in the cooking liquid. The simplicity of this preparation allows the flavor of the potato to take precedence, with a subtle backup from the olive oil (don't be afraid to use an assertive, early-harvest olive oil here).

Mashed Potatoes

SERVES 4 TO 6

3 pounds potatoes, such as russet, peeled and
cut into 1½-inch chunks
3 teaspoons sea salt or kosher salt
1 cup whole milk, plus extra if needed
4 tablespoons unsalted butter
Freshly ground white pepper

1. In a 4- to 6-quart saucepan, combine the potatoes
with water to cover. Place over medium-high heat,
add ½ teaspoon of the salt, and bring to a boil.
Meanwhile, in a small saucepan, combine the
milk and butter and heat until the milk scalds
(tiny bubbles appear around the edge of the pan)
but does not boil. Keep warm. Reduce the heat
under the potatoes to maintain a simmer and cook
until they are just done; start testing after 10 minutes. You should be able to pierce them with a
skewer or knife with only slight resistance.

2. When the potatoes are ready, drain well. While
they are still hot, pass them through a potato
ricer or the medium screen of a food mill placed
over a warmed bowl. Sprinkle them with the
remaining 2½ teaspoons salt and add most of the
milk-butter mixture and a few turns of the pepper
grinder. Stir just until combined. Taste and adjust
the seasoning, and add more of the milk-butter
mixture if the potatoes are too thick. Stir the
potatoes only enough to mix in the liquid and
seasonings. If stirred too much, the potatoes will
become thick and glutinous and lose their airy
texture. Serve at once.

Potato Purée

SERVES 4 TO 6

3 pounds waxy potatoes such as Yukon Gold or
Yellow Finn, peeled and cut into 1½-inch chunks
1½ teaspoons sea salt or kosher salt
⅓ cup extra virgin olive oil
½ cup whole milk, warmed
¼ teaspoon freshly ground pepper (optional)

1. In a 3-quart saucepan, combine the potatoes with
water to cover. Place over medium-high heat, add
the salt, and bring to a boil. Reduce the heat to
maintain a simmer and cook the potatoes until
they are just done; start testing after 10 minutes.
You should be able to pierce them with a skewer
or a knife with only slight resistance. (Not
allowing potatoes to boil after they are initially
brought to temperature will do much to improve
their flavor and texture.)

2. When the potatoes are ready, drain well, reserving the cooking liquid. While they are still hot,
pass them through a ricer or the medium screen
of a food mill into a bowl set over a saucepan
of simmering water. Using a spoon, mix in the
olive oil and milk. While continuing to mix,
work in ¼ cup of the reserved cooking water,
then add enough additional cooking water as
needed to make a fairly soft, creamy purée. Stir
in the pepper (if using), then taste and adjust
the seasoning. Serve at once.

Polenta

SERVES 4 TO 6 *Polenta, a versatile northern Italian cornmeal dish, complements many different foods. I particularly like to serve it alongside rabbit, fowl, and pork preparations that have plenty of sauce or juice. The flavorful meat liquids mix with the starchiness of the polenta to create a delicious match. Polenta can be served with most sauces meant for pasta, too, particularly those based on tomato such as Tomato Sauce (page 84) or Italian Sausage and Tomato Sauce (page 85). Soft polenta can also be mixed with cheese— mozzarella, Parmesan, or Gorgonzola—to taste, sprinkled with a few toasted walnuts, and served as a wonderful first course. Do not substitute regular cornmeal for polenta as the textures are different.*

4 cups water

1 cup coarse-grind polenta

1 teaspoon sea salt or kosher salt

1. Bring the water to a full rolling boil in a heavy-bottomed 2- or 3-quart saucepan. Using a wooden spoon, stir the water vigorously while pouring the polenta in a steady stream into the water. Continue stirring constantly over high heat. When the polenta thickens and large bubbles begin to form and pop on the surface, after 1 to 2 minutes, reduce the heat to medium. Continue stirring constantly, being careful to scrape the bottom of the pan clean. As the polenta thickens further and the bubbles begin to splatter, reduce the heat to low. At this point the polenta should be thick enough to hold soft, low mounds on its surface. Cover the pot with a tight-fitting lid, reduce the heat to very low, and cook, stirring occasionally, until thickened, about 45 minutes. Stir in the salt and adjust the consistency with water as needed. I like to serve polenta fairly soft. It should pour from a spoon, but just barely.

Allow to cook for another 10 minutes, then taste and adjust the seasoning. Serve piping hot.

2. To serve the polenta grilled, sautéed, or baked, turn the hot polenta out into a lightly buttered 8-by-12-inch baking pan. Smooth the surface and allow the polenta to cool, then refrigerate until thoroughly chilled, about 2 hours. Cut into serving portions. To grill, brush very lightly with olive oil and grill over a hot natural-charcoal fire. For best results, do not attempt to turn the polenta over until it has formed a good crust. To sauté, using tongs, carefully lower pieces into a hot pan that has been filmed with olive oil and cook briskly until a crust forms. Using a spatula, turn the pieces over carefully and cook the other side. To bake, arrange the pieces on a lightly oiled, rimmed baking sheet and place in a 350°F oven until heated through, about 15 minutes. You can also put the pieces in an oiled earthenware baking dish, cover with the sauce of your choice, and top with grated cheese. Cooked in this manner, the polenta will take about 30 minutes to heat.

Desserts

Just about everyone loves a little something sweet to end a meal, or to accompany an afternoon cup of coffee or tea. It does not have to be layers high and filled with buttercream. It just has to be good.

Here at the ranch, I don't have to look far for ideas. A Black Mission fig tree that shades the deck outside the kitchen yields sweet fruits that get combined with our own walnuts for Fig-Walnut Tart (page 158). I also like to serve the figs simply cut in half, arranged on a plate with some fresh goat cheese, and then drizzled with lavender honey. When berry season arrives, Margaret and her crew present us with an astonishing array of sweet berries—black, red, and golden raspberries, red currants, strawberries, and more—that are served just as they are or made into sorbets, ice creams, and fruit sauces.

Good olive oil has its place in baking, too. Our Walnut–Olive Oil Cake (page 156), Olio Nuovo and Lemon Cookies (page 154), and Chocolate–Olive Oil Cookies (page 153) garner rave reviews from visitors and ranch staff alike.

Lemon Biscotti

MAKES ABOUT 36 COOKIES *Cookies are a favorite at the ranch. We serve them at some of the tours that are conducted for visitors and, of course, for dessert. These have a sprightly flavor thanks to fresh lemon zest, lemon oil, and a good splash of lemon-flavored vodka, which you can easily make at home or buy. Once the vodka has steeped, I like to store it in the freezer: the flavor stays fresh, and the vodka is always ready for making a great-tasting martini. Pure lemon oil is just that, oil extracted from lemon zest, rather than lemon extract, which is lemon oil mixed with alcohol. It is perishable, however, so always store it in the refrigerator.*

1½ cups unbleached all-purpose flour

1½ cups yellow cornmeal

¼ teaspoon baking powder

¼ teaspoon sea salt or kosher salt

½ cup unsalted butter, at room temperature

⅔ cup sugar

2 large egg yolks

1 tablespoon grated lemon zest

¼ teaspoon pure lemon oil such as Boyajian brand

¼ cup Lemon Vodka (page 152)

1. Sift together the flour, cornmeal, baking powder, and salt into a medium-sized bowl. In a large bowl, using a hand mixer at high speed, cream together the butter and sugar until light in color, about 2 minutes. Add the egg yolks one at a time, mixing well after each addition. Mix in the lemon zest, lemon oil, and vodka. Using a wooden spoon or the hand mixer at low speed, add the sifted dry ingredients, mixing well. Cover the dough with plastic wrap and refrigerate for 30 minutes.

2. Preheat the oven to 350°F. Butter a baking sheet and dust it lightly with cornmeal, or line it with a silicone baking sheet.

continued

3. Divide the dough in half. Using your hands and working on a lightly floured surface, form each half into a log 9 inches long by 1 1/4 inches in diameter. Place the logs on the prepared baking sheet, spacing them well apart (they will spread during baking). Bake the logs for 30 minutes. They will be very pale in color.

4. Remove the baking sheet from the oven, and reduce the oven heat to 300°F. When the logs are cool enough to handle, transfer them to a cutting board and cut on the diagonal into slices 1/2 inch thick. Place the slices cut side down on the baking sheet.

5. Return the baking sheet to the oven and bake the cookies for 15 minutes. Turn them over and continue baking until lightly browned, about 10 minutes longer. Transfer the cookies to a wire rack and let cool completely. Store in an airtight container at room temperature for up to 1 week.

Lemon Vodka

Using a vegetable peeler and working in a spiral from one end to the other (a few breaks won't matter, but try to remove as little of the white pith as possible), remove the zest from 3 organic lemons. Poke the strips into an almost-full bottle of good-quality vodka (the zest will displace some of the vodka so you cannot start with a full one). Cap the bottle and leave it in a dark place for 3 to 4 weeks before using.

Chocolate-Olive Oil Cookies

MAKES ABOUT 60 COOKIES *These cookies are an interesting variation on the lemon cookies on page 154, and it's a nice idea to serve them together. Their flavor is reminiscent of Mexican chocolate. They can also be frozen and then baked when needed. See the introduction to the lemon cookies for directions on freezing.*

1²⁄₃ cups unbleached all-purpose flour

1 cup sugar

¹⁄₃ cup unsweetened cocoa powder, plus extra
   for dusting

¹⁄₂ teaspoon baking soda

1 teaspoon ground cinnamon

³⁄₄ cup extra virgin olive oil

1 teaspoon vanilla extract

¹⁄₄ teaspoon almond extract

3 ounces bittersweet chocolate, melted and cooled
   to barely lukewarm

1. Preheat the oven to 350°F. Line 2 large baking sheets with baking parchment or silicone baking sheets.

2. Sift together the flour, sugar, ¹⁄₃ cup cocoa powder, baking soda, and cinnamon into a medium-sized bowl. In a small bowl, stir together the olive oil and vanilla and almond extracts, then add to the dry ingredients. Add the melted chocolate and stir until the mixture comes together into a uniform mass. Using your hands, roll the dough into balls ³⁄₄ to 1 inch in diameter and place them on the prepared baking sheets, spacing them 2 inches apart.

3. Bake the cookies 1 sheet at a time until cooked through and very lightly browned, about 15 minutes. Transfer to a wire rack and let cool completely. Store in an airtight container at room temperature for up to 3 days. Dust lightly with cocoa powder before serving.

Olio Nuovo and Lemon Cookies

MAKES ABOUT 60 COOKIES *These cookies, which are reminiscent of Mexican wedding cookies or Russian tea cakes, were created to showcase the wonderful zesty freshness of our olio nuovo, or "new oil," which is available for only a few weeks immediately after harvest in the fall. However, don't worry if olio nuovo season has passed, as these cookies are still excellent made with any full-flavored early-harvest olive oil. Tuscan extra virgin olive oils and McEvoy Ranch extra virgin olive oil, which are made when the fruit is still fairly green, are two examples of early-harvest oils. I also enjoy these cookies flavored with orange. Simply substitute navel orange zest, orange oil, and orange juice where appropriate.*

If you do not want to bake all the cookies at one time, you can freeze part of the batch unbaked for up to 3 months. Arrange the balls, without touching, on a baking sheet, and freeze until hard. Then transfer the frozen balls to a zippered freezer bag and place in the freezer until needed. When you want to bake the cookies, they can go straight into the oven, although they might need a few extra minutes of baking time.

2 cups unbleached all-purpose flour

1 cup sugar

½ teaspoon baking soda

¾ cup *olio nuovo*

⅛ teaspoon pure lemon oil such as Boyajian brand

4 teaspoons grated lemon zest

1 teaspoon fresh lemon juice

1. Preheat the oven to 350°F. Line 2 large baking sheets with baking parchment or silicone baking sheets.

2. Sift together the flour, sugar, and baking soda into a medium-sized bowl. In a small bowl, stir together the olive oil, lemon oil, lemon zest, and lemon juice. Add the wet ingredients to the dry ingredients, then stir until the mixture comes together into a uniform mass. Using your hands, roll the dough into balls ¾ to 1 inch in diameter, and place them on the prepared baking sheets, spacing them 2 inches apart.

3. Bake the cookies 1 sheet at a time until cooked through and very lightly browned, about 15 minutes. Transfer to a wire rack and let cool completely. Store in an airtight container at room temperature for up to 3 days.

Walnut-Olive Oil Cake

SERVES 8 TO 12 *The Mediterranean region has a long history of desserts made with olive oil. This light and flavorful cake was inspired by that tradition. I like to serve it in spring and early summer with a dusting of confectioners' sugar and strawberries bruised with a little sugar.*

¾ cup walnut halves and pieces
1½ cups unbleached all-purpose flour
2 teaspoons baking powder
Pinch of sea salt or kosher salt
3 large eggs
¾ cup plus 2 tablespoons granulated sugar
⅓ cup extra virgin olive oil
⅓ cup Italian walnut liqueur such as Nocetto, or,
 if unavailable, Amaretto
Confectioners' sugar for dusting
Lightly sweetened strawberries and/or whipped cream
 for serving

1. Preheat the oven to 325°F. Generously butter a 9-inch round cake pan.

2. Spread the walnuts on a baking sheet and toast until very lightly colored, about 5 minutes. Remove from the oven and let stand until cool enough to handle. Pour onto a clean kitchen towel and rub the nuts to remove as much of their tannic, papery membrane as you can. Turn into a colander and shake to remove any of the remaining membrane that is easily dislodged. Transfer the walnuts to a cutting board and, using a sharp knife, finely chop them and set aside. Increase the oven temperature to 350°F.

3. Sift together the flour, baking powder, and salt into a bowl; repeat the sifting twice more. In a stand mixer, beat the eggs on high speed until light in color, about 2 minutes. Gradually add the sugar and beat until the mixture is pale and thick, about 4 minutes longer. Reduce the speed to low and mix in the olive oil and liqueur. Remove the bowl from the stand.

4. Using a rubber spatula, lightly fold the flour mixture into the egg mixture in 3 batches. Fold the walnuts into the batter. Pour the mixture into the prepared pan and smooth the surface.

5. Bake the cake until the top springs back lightly when touched and a toothpick comes out *just* clean, 35 to 40 minutes. It is important not to overbake this cake, or it will become dry. Transfer to a wire rack and let cool in the pan for 10 minutes. Turn the cake out onto the rack and let cool completely.

6. Place the cake on a serving plate and dust the top lightly with the confectioners' sugar. Serve with strawberries and/or whipped cream.

Pie or Tart Dough

MAKES DOUGH FOR ONE 8- OR 9-INCH DOUBLE-CRUST TART OR PIE *My mother was famous for the crisp flakiness of her pie crust, but I like this dough even more than hers due to the extra flavor from the butter (she used all shortening). Be sure to leave a lot of the butter pieces large to create a crust that is full of crispy flakes. I like to bake this dough to a medium brown, which requires a longer baking time than what is called for in many recipes. Baking to color rather than time will ensure that the dough is not undercooked, which accentuates the nutty flavor of the pastry and also reduces any starchiness in the filling. If the day is a warm one, it is a good idea to freeze the mixer bowl, paddle, and flour together for an hour or so before mixing the dough. This will allow the butter pieces to remain whole, rather than melt during mixing. The well-wrapped disks of dough can be frozen for up to 6 months.*

2 cups unbleached all-purpose flour

Rounded ¼ teaspoon sea salt or kosher salt

½ teaspoon sugar

6 tablespoons unsalted butter, chilled, cut into bean-sized pieces

4 tablespoons salted butter, chilled, cut into bean-sized pieces

4 tablespoons shortening, chilled

3 ½ tablespoons ice water

1. In the bowl of a stand mixer, combine the flour, salt, and sugar and stir with a spoon to mix. Fit the mixer with the paddle attachment and add the unsalted butter, salted butter, and shortening. Mix on low speed until the mixture has the consistency of coarse meal with quite a few larger pieces in it. Add the ice water all at once and mix just until combined.

2. Divide the dough into 2 equal portions and flatten each portion into a 5-inch disk. Wrap the disks separately in plastic wrap and refrigerate for at least 30 minutes or for up to 24 hours before rolling out.

Fig-Walnut Tart

MAKES TWO 8-INCH TARTS; SERVES 16 *This is one of the first desserts that I created after coming to the ranch, and it has been described as the best Fig Newton you will ever taste! It was inspired by views from the kitchen windows: on one side is a gnarled old Black Mission fig tree that produces a bountiful crop each year that we eat both fresh and dried; on the other side is a deck shaded by a walnut tree. In the fall when the nuts ripen, we gather them and save them to shell on rainy winter days. This tart is fairly unusual in that it has both a top and a bottom crust.*

Double recipe Pie or Tart Dough (page 157)

1 cup walnut halves and pieces
3 cups tightly packed dried figs, preferably Black
    Mission, stems removed and coarsely chopped
½ cup late-harvest Gewürztraminer or other sweet
    dessert wine
Zest of 1 orange, preferably navel, grated or removed
    with a zester
½ cup firmly packed light brown sugar
½ cup honey
¼ teaspoon pure orange oil such as Boyajian brand
3 large egg yolks
¾ cup heavy cream
1 large egg yolk mixed with 1 teaspoon milk for
    egg wash
Granulated sugar for sprinkling
Lightly sweetened whipped cream or Blood Orange
    Frozen Yogurt (page 170) for serving

1. Prepare the tart dough as directed, and refrigerate the 4 dough disks until needed.

2. Preheat the oven to 325°F. Spread the walnuts on a baking sheet and toast until very lightly colored, about 5 minutes. Remove from the oven and let stand until cool enough to handle, then pour onto a clean kitchen towel and rub the nuts to remove as much of their tannic, papery membrane as you can. Turn into a colander and shake to remove any of the remaining membrane that is easily dislodged. Set the walnuts aside.

3. Increase the oven temperature to 425°F. Combine the figs and wine in a glass bowl, cover loosely with plastic wrap, and microwave on low power for 3 minutes to soften. Alternatively, in a small covered pan over low heat, simmer the figs and wine together for 3 minutes, turn off the heat, and allow to stand, still covered, for 5 minutes.

4. Add the walnuts and orange zest to the fig mixture. Transfer to a food processor and pulse to form a mixture with the texture of mincemeat, or pass through a food grinder fitted with the large disk. Set aside.

continued

5. In a large bowl, stir together the brown sugar, honey, orange oil, egg yolks, and cream until combined. Add the fig-walnut mixture and mix thoroughly. Set aside.

6. On a lightly floured work surface, roll out the dough disks to a thickness of $^1/8$ inch, or a little thicker. Cut two of them into 11-inch circles and two of them into 9-inch circles. Line 2 round 8-inch tart pans with removable bottoms and 1-inch sides with the larger circles, gently pressing the dough into the bottom and sides, and paying particular attention to the angle where the sides meet the base. Divide the filling evenly between the pastry-lined pans and level with a spatula. Brush the edges of the dough with the egg wash. Top the filled pans with the smaller dough circles. Run a rolling pin across the top of each pan to seal the edges together and trim off the excess dough. Brush the tops with egg wash and sprinkle with granulated sugar.

7. Bake the tarts for 20 minutes. Reduce the heat to 375°F and continue to bake until the tops are golden brown, 20 to 30 minutes longer. Transfer to a wire rack and let cool to room temperature. Remove the sides of the tart pans, leaving the tarts on the pan bases. Cut into wedges, and serve with whipped cream or frozen yogurt.

Yogurt and Fruit Scones

MAKES 16 SCONES *This is my version of a butterless scone, which is more cakelike than a traditional scone. For the dried fruit, I use raisins, currants, blueberries, or a mix of all three, or I use one of my favorite combinations, dried cherries and golden raisins. The yogurt can be nonfat, low-fat, or whole milk, according to the degree of richness desired. Serve the scones with some homemade jam or marmalade, and with coffee, tea, or a glass of cold milk.*

2 cups unbleached all-purpose flour
1 tablespoon baking powder
¼ teaspoon baking soda
½ teaspoon sea salt or kosher salt
¼ cup sugar
¾ cup dried fruit (see recipe introduction)
1 cup plain yogurt
1 large egg
2 tablespoons canola oil or corn oil

1. Preheat the oven to 425°F. Have ready an ungreased baking sheet.

2. Sift together the flour, baking powder, baking soda, salt, and sugar into a large bowl. Stir in the dried fruit. In a small bowl, stir together the yogurt, egg, and oil, then fold into the flour mixture just until combined.

3. Turn the dough out onto a lightly floured board, knead a few times, and divide in half. Pat each half into a circle about 10 inches in diameter and ³/₄ inch thick. Make sure the bottoms of the circles have an ample coating of flour, and transfer the circles to the baking sheet. Cut each circle into 8 wedges and separate slightly.

4. Bake the scones until lightly browned, about 15 minutes. Transfer to a wire rack and let cool for a few minutes, then serve warm.

VARIATION: *Add ¹/₂ cup walnuts or hazelnuts, lightly toasted, skinned as described on page 156 (the method works for hazelnuts, too), and chopped, with the dried fruit.*

Lavender Ice Cream

MAKES 1½ QUARTS *For me, the real charm of this dessert lies in using fresh lavender flowers, but dried will still make an aromatic ice cream. Be sure to use Lavandula angustifolia—not all lavender species are suitable for cooking.*

1 tablespoon fresh lavender flowers
(*Lavandula angustifolia*), or 1½ tablespoons
dried lavender flowers

3 lemon zest strips, each about 2 inches long
and ½ inch wide

3 cups half-and-half

1 cup heavy cream

8 large egg yolks

¾ cup sugar

1 teaspoon vanilla extract

3 tablespoons fresh lemon juice

1. In a 2-quart saucepan, combine the lavender, lemon zest, half-and-half, and cream and bring to a simmer over medium heat, stirring often. Remove from the heat, cover, and leave to infuse for 1 hour.

2. In a bowl, combine the egg yolks, sugar, and vanilla and whisk until pale and thick, about 2 minutes. Uncover the lavender-cream infusion, return to the stove top, and bring back to a simmer. Whisk ½ cup of the hot cream mixture into the yolk-sugar mixture and, while whisking constantly, pour it all back into cream mixture. Continue cooking over medium heat, stirring constantly, until the custard thickens enough to coat a wooden spoon or registers 185°F on an instant-read thermometer, 3 to 4 minutes. Do not allow the custard to boil or it will curdle. Remove from the heat and immediately pour through a fine-mesh sieve into a clean bowl. Place the bowl in a larger bowl of ice water and allow to chill thoroughly, stirring occasionally. Stir in the lemon juice, cover, and refrigerate until ready to freeze.

3. Pour the chilled custard into an ice cream maker and freeze according to the manufacturer's instructions.

Mint Julep Ice Cream

MAKES 1 1/2 QUARTS *Mark likes to serve this clean, refreshing treat in Pistachio Tuiles (page 166), which he then garnishes with some fresh berries and a fresh mint sprig or a few edible flowers.*

3 cups whole milk
1 cup heavy cream
1 bunch fresh mint, stems removed and leaves
    chopped
7 large egg yolks
3/4 cup sugar
3 tablespoons bourbon

1. In a 2-quart saucepan, combine the milk and cream and bring to a simmer over medium heat. Add the mint, stir well, and remove from the heat. Let cool and then transfer to an airtight container. Let steep in the refrigerator for at least 6 hours or for up to overnight.

2. In a bowl, combine the yolks and sugar and whisk until pale and thick, about 2 minutes. Remove the mint mixture from the refrigerator and strain through a fine-mesh sieve into a clean saucepan. Discard the mint. Place the saucepan over medium heat and bring to a simmer, stirring often. Whisk 1/2 cup of the hot milk mixture into the yolk-sugar mixture and, while whisking constantly, pour it all back into the milk mixture. Continue cooking over medium heat, stirring constantly, until the custard thickens enough to coat a wooden spoon or registers 185°F on an instant-read thermometer, 3 to 4 minutes. Do not allow the custard to boil or it will curdle. Remove from the heat and immediately pour through a fine-mesh sieve into a clean bowl. Place the bowl into a larger bowl of ice water and allow to chill thoroughly, stirring occasionally. Stir in the bourbon, cover, and refrigerate until ready to freeze.

3. Pour the chilled custard into an ice cream maker and freeze according to the manufacturer's instructions.

VARIATION: *To make lemon verbena ice cream, substitute 1 cup loosely packed fresh lemon verbena leaves for the mint, substitute Lemon Vodka (page 152) for the bourbon, and shorten the steeping time to 2 hours.*

Fresh Strawberry Gelée

LINES 6 TO 8 PLATES, OR MAKES 2 CUPS CUBES *I have always had a soft spot for Jell-O and occasionally like to use a more sophisticated version of it as a textural contrast in dishes. Margaret's strawberries have an incredibly intense aroma and flavor, and really shine when prepared in this manner. As a "mirror" on a plate, the gel makes a delectable visual counterpoint to a dessert placed on top of it, such as fresh fruit or a slice of almond tart. As cubes, the strawberry gel, along with some toasted sliced almonds, is wonderful folded into tapioca pudding flavored with Grand Marnier or scattered on top of fresh fruit. Try the same ratio of gelatin to liquid with other fruit juices and purées to make gels or cubes. Or, if you prefer, you can add up to double the quantity of gelatin to make a firmer gel. Do not use pineapple or kiwifruit unless you cook it first; cooking destroys an enzyme that interferes with the setting process.*

2 cups ripe, fragrant strawberries, hulled

6 tablespoons sugar

¼ teaspoon vanilla extract

1 tablespoon fresh lemon juice

¼ cup water

1 envelope (¼ ounce) unflavored gelatin

1. In a food processor, combine the strawberries, sugar, vanilla, and lemon juice and process to form a smooth purée. Pour the purée into a bowl, straining all or part of the mixture through a fine-mesh sieve if you do not like strawberry seeds. Put the water in a small saucepan and sprinkle the gelatin evenly over the surface. Allow to stand undisturbed for 5 minutes. Place the pan over low heat and swirl until the gelatin has dissolved. Scrape the dissolved gelatin into the strawberry mixture and stir well to combine.

2. To line plates or bowls, carefully ladle out enough of the strawberry mixture to create a coating about 3/8 inch thick on the bottoms of white dessert plates or bowls, then refrigerate until set, about 45 minutes. (Plates often have a small inner rim that can act as a natural dam to hold the liquid in place.)

3. To make cubes, line a 6- to 8-inch square baking pan with plastic wrap and pour in the strawberry mixture. Refrigerate until set, about 1 hour. Turn out the gelled square onto a clean work surface and peel off the plastic wrap. Using a sharp knife, cut into 3/8-inch cubes.

Pistachio Tuiles

MAKES 12 TO 15 TUILES *Cookies and ice cream is a classic combination that the French have made even better by forming the cookie into a cup and putting the ice cream inside. Mark has given these crunchy cups a colorful twist by sprinkling them with pistachios, although sliced almonds or another chopped nut can also be used. Forming the tuiles is easier than it sounds. The important thing to remember is to work quickly because they rapidly become crisp as they cool. Mark likes to shape them by draping them over the tops of empty McEvoy olive oil bottles. You can also drape them over inverted ramekins, press them inside slightly larger ramekins or bowls, or roll them around a wooden spoon handle to form a tube. If the humidity is high, the tuiles will not keep well and should be served the same day they are made.*

To serve ice cream in a tuile cup, put a small dab of ice cream in the center of a chilled dessert plate. Place the tuile on the ice cream, which will keep it from sliding, and fill the tuile with scoops of ice cream. Garnish with something appropriate to the ice cream, such as fresh fruit if using fruit ice cream, or just about anything if using vanilla ice cream. Lightly sweetened whipped cream is rarely out of place with any ice cream. Candied Walnuts (page 172) are good with vanilla, chocolate, and many fruit ice creams. Don't be afraid to try different combinations.

½ cup unbleached bread flour
½ cup confectioners' sugar
Pinch of sea salt or kosher salt
3 tablespoons unsalted butter, melted
3 large egg whites
½ teaspoon vanilla extract
½ cup unsalted pistachios, finely chopped

1. Preheat the oven to 400°F. Spray a baking sheet with nonstick cooking spray or line with a silicone baking sheet.

2. Sift together the flour, sugar, and salt into a small bowl. With a fork, stir in the melted butter. Place the egg whites in another small bowl and whisk in the vanilla. Whisk the egg white–vanilla mixture into the flour mixture until thoroughly combined (a few lumps are fine). Drop 1 tablespoon of the batter onto the prepared baking sheet and, using the back of the tablespoon or a small offset spatula, shape the batter into a circle 3 to 4 inches in diameter and of uniform thickness. Sprinkle with the pistachios.

3. This first tuile is a test to see if the consistency of the batter is right. Put the pan in the oven and bake until the outside rim of the cookie—a border at least $3/4$ inch wide—is golden, 5 to 7 minutes. The center will remain paler and more malleable. Remove the pan from the oven and, using a long, thin spatula, quickly lift off the cookie and invert it, pistachio side down, onto whatever object you have chosen for shaping the tuile. (If you are forming your tuile inside a bowl or ramekin, put the pistachio side facing up.) Gently shape the tuile and leave it in place for 30 to 60 seconds to set. If the tuile seems too thick, thin the batter with a little milk; start with $1/2$ teaspoon. When you are satisfied with the consistency, you can cook 2 tuiles at a time, letting the 2 shaped tuiles cool while you are forming the next pair.

4. Serve the tuiles immediately or keep in an airtight container for up to 2 days.

Frozen Yogurt

I love homemade frozen yogurts because, with higher acidity and lower fat than ice cream, they are wonderfully fresh and clean tasting. I have given four examples here but there are many more possibilities. If you like the taste of these, experiment with some others. Pineapple, other berries, and citrus fruits are all good when prepared in this manner.

People often ask me if they should use whole, low-fat, or nonfat milk yogurt when making frozen yogurt desserts. The answer is that all of them will work just fine and give creamy results, but in a decreasing order of richness.

The amount of sugar to use depends on the sweetness of the fruit. For the recipes included here, I've suggested from $^{1}/_{2}$ to $1^{1}/_{2}$ cups as a starting point, but it's important to taste the mixture as you go along and add more sugar if necessary. Remember, it should taste slightly too sweet at this point because you need to counteract the tendency for sweetness to become less pronounced at lower temperatures. A frozen yogurt will always be creamier than an ice milk made with an equivalent butterfat content, a condition partially explained by the additional sugar needed to counteract the yogurt's extra acidity.

Strawberry Frozen Yogurt

MAKES ABOUT 1¹/2 QUARTS

5 cups ripe, fragrant strawberries, hulled
1¼ cups sugar, or as needed
3 tablespoons fresh lemon juice
1 teaspoon vanilla extract
1 quart plain yogurt

In a food processor, pulse the strawberries to make a slightly rough purée. Add the 1¼ cups sugar, the lemon juice, vanilla, and yogurt and process until well combined and the sugar has dissolved. Taste and add more sugar if needed. Pour into an ice cream maker and freeze according to the manufacturer's instructions.

Lemon Frozen Yogurt

MAKES ABOUT 1¹/2 QUARTS

Zest of 3 lemons, removed with a vegetable peeler
1½ cups sugar, or as needed
1¼ cups fresh lemon juice
2 cups plain yogurt

In a food processor, combine the lemon zest and 1¹/2 cups sugar and process to pulverize the zest and coat the sugar with its oils, about 3 minutes. Add the lemon juice and yogurt and process until the sugar has dissolved. Taste and add more sugar if needed. Pour into an ice cream maker and freeze according to the manufacturer's instructions.

continued

Nectarine Frozen Yogurt

MAKES ABOUT 1 1/2 QUARTS

2 pounds ripe, fragrant nectarines, halved and pitted

1/2 cup sugar, or as needed

1/2 teaspoon vanilla extract

1/4 teaspoon almond extract

2 cups plain yogurt

In a food processor, combine the nectarines, 1/2 cup sugar, and the vanilla and almond extracts and pulse to make a slightly rough purée. Add the yogurt and process until well combined and the sugar has dissolved. Taste and add more sugar if needed. Pour into an ice cream maker and freeze according to the manufacturer's instructions.

Blood Orange Frozen Yogurt

MAKES ABOUT 1 1/2 QUARTS

2 cups fresh blood orange juice

1 cup sugar, or as needed

1 tablespoon Cointreau

1/2 teaspoon vanilla extract

1 teaspoon grated blood orange zest

1 quart plain yogurt

In a bowl, whisk together the orange juice, 1 cup sugar, the Cointreau, vanilla, orange zest, and yogurt until the sugar has dissolved. Taste and add more sugar if needed. Pour into an ice cream maker and freeze according to the manufacturer's instructions.

Candied Walnuts

MAKES 1½ CUPS *These nuts make an exceptional topping for ice creams, and are equally good as part of a farmhouse cheese and fresh fruit selection or with salads containing fruit or fruit vinaigrettes, such as the Spiced Pork Tenderloin with Cherries and Sweet Spices served as a salad (page 112).*

1½ cups walnut halves
¼ cup sugar
⅛ teaspoon sea salt or kosher salt

1. Preheat the oven to 325°F. Spread the walnuts on a baking sheet and toast until very lightly colored, about 5 minutes. Remove from the oven and let stand until cool enough to handle, then pour onto a clean kitchen towel and rub the nuts to remove as much of their tannic, papery membrane as you can. Turn into a colander and shake to remove any of the remaining membrane that is easily dislodged.

2. Put the sugar in a sauté pan over medium heat. Cook, shaking the pan by the handle but not stirring the contents, until the sugar melts and has turned a medium-brown caramel color. Add the walnuts and stir with a wooden spoon to coat them with the caramel. Scrape out onto a surface covered with a silicone baking sheet, onto a marble slab, or onto a lightly buttered baking sheet. While the nuts are still hot, use 2 forks to separate them as best you can. Sprinkle with the salt and let cool. Use immediately, or store in an airtight container at room temperature. If the humidity is fairly low, the nuts will keep for up to 1 week.

Index

Acknowledgments

THE RANCH EXISTS DUE TO THE PRESCIENCE OF Nan McEvoy, who saw Xanadu in a glimpse of an old dairy ranch from a distant road. Her vision and determination have created a wonderful enclave in this little valley by finding a few good people and giving them rein to do what they do. I am proud to be part of this team. Both my presence on the team and my possession of the skills necessary to be on it are due, in large measure, to Joyce Goldstein, who connected me with Nan McEvoy and who provided the place, her restaurant Square One, where I learned immeasurably about food and cooking.

This book could not have been written, and indeed the ranch could not operate, without the support of the McEvoy Ranch staff. Heartfelt thanks go to each one of them: the ones who are our public faces, who lead tours, do tastings, and answer phones, as well as those who labor so tirelessly in the olive orchards, gardens, and buildings.

Special thanks go to orchard manager Shari DeJoseph, whose thoughtful nurturing of the olive trees results in incomparable fruit; head gardener Margaret Koski-Kent, who coaxes outstanding organic produce, flowers, and overall beauty from the gardens with aplomb, whose unparalleled eye for color and design are responsible for the most beautiful and outrageous flower arrangements I have ever seen, and whose friendship and palate are so vital to my work here; chef Mark Rohrmeier, who has given us countless great meals, who ably wears many other hats besides his chef's toque, and who has willingly held up my end of things during the production of this work; general contractor Russ Morita, who has been in charge of all construction on the ranch almost since its inception, regularly achieving the impossible, and who is the father of our ranch family and a great friend; Jeffrey Creque, agricultural ecologist, *frantoio* supervisor, and overseer of the ranch's organic program, whose serene competence is a model to us all; journeyman olive oil maker José Chavez, the rock on which our oil production is based, who completed his four-year apprenticeship at the McEvoy *frantoio* in 2003; machine-shop supervisor Michael Morelli, who grew up on this land and has acted as an invaluable owner's manual, providing generations of knowledge about the ranch (Michael is a direct descendant of previous owners of the ranch; his Swiss Italian great-grandmother arrived here in 1880 as a bride); housekeeping supervisor Joan Cupoletti, who keeps the workplace spotless in the middle of a working ranch; and olive oil production consultant Dr. Maurizio Castelli, whose ongoing advice and expertise remain so vital and whose palate, nose, and friendship are immeasurably important to us.

Extra-special thanks to coauthor Jacqueline Mallorca, whose competence and experience have been invaluable throughout this process; to Chronicle Books editor Bill LeBlond, whose enthusiasm and guidance have been crucial; and to talented photographer Maren Caruso, who captured the essence of the ranch and who, along with assistant Faiza Ali and food stylists Erin Quon and Kim Konecny, have made our food look so beautiful.

Finally, on the home front, very special thanks go to my wife, Joan Sullivan, whose idea it was that I go to cooking school, for her love, patience, invaluable editing assistance, and, most important, for being the most wonderful mother to our beautiful daughters, Julia and Rosemary.

—*Gerald Gass*

Table of Equivalents

The exact equivalents in the following tables have been rounded for convenience.

liquid/dry measures

u.s.	metric
$^1/_4$ teaspoon	1.25 milliliters
$^1/_2$ teaspoon	2.5 milliliters
1 teaspoon	5 milliliters
1 tablespoon (3 teaspoons)	15 milliliters
1 fluid ounce (2 tablespoons)	30 milliliters
$^1/_4$ cup	60 milliliters
$^1/_3$ cup	80 milliliters
$^1/_2$ cup	120 milliliters
1 cup	240 milliliters
1 pint (2 cups)	480 milliliters
1 quart (4 cups, 32 ounces)	960 milliliters
1 gallon (4 quarts)	3.84 liters
1 ounce (by weight)	28 grams
1 pound	454 grams
2.2 pounds	1 kilogram

length

u.s.	metric
$^1/_8$ inch	3 millimeters
$^1/_4$ inch	6 millimeters
$^1/_2$ inch	12 millimeters
1 inch	2.5 centimeters

oven temperature

fahrenheit	celsius	gas
250	120	$^1/_2$
275	140	1
300	150	2
325	160	3
350	180	4
375	190	5
400	200	6
425	220	7
450	230	8
475	240	9
500	260	10